岸本斉史

I'm starting to run out of things to write for this "Author's Comments" section...
Since going to the movies is practically my only hobby, I guess I'll write about movies...
Hmm. Some movies I've seen recently are...
...Oh man! I've been so busy recently that I haven't gone to the movies--!!
I want to see movies...

—Masashi Kishimoto, 2002

Author/artist Masashi Kishimoto was born in 1974 in rural Okayama Prefecture, Japan. After spending time in art college, he won the Hop Step Award for new manga artists with his manga **Karakuri** (Mechanism). Kishimoto decided to base his next story on traditional Japanese culture. His first version of **Naruto**, drawn in 1997, was a one-shot story about fox spirits; his final version, which debuted in **Weekly Shonen Jump** in 1999, quickly became the most popular ninja manga in Japan.

NARUTO VOL. 15
The SHONEN JUMP Manga Edition

This graphic novel contains material that was originally published in English in **SHONEN JUMP** #54-55.

STORY AND ART BY MASASHI KISHIMOTO

Translation & English Adaptation/Mari Morimoto
Touch-up Art & Lettering/Inori Fukuda Trant
Additional Touch-up/Josh Simpson
Design/Sean Lee
Editor//Joel Enos

Editor in Chief, Books/Alvin Lu
Editor in Chief, Magazines/Marc Weidenbaum
VP of Publishing Licensing/Rika Inouye
VP of Sales/Gonzalo Ferreyra
Sr. VP of Marketing/Liza Coppola
Publisher/Hyoe Narita

Printed in the U.S.A.

Published by VIZ Media, LLC
P.O. Box 77010
San Francisco, CA 94107

SHONEN JUMP Manga Edition
10 9 8 7 6 5 4 3 2 1
First printing, July 2007

SHONEN JUMP MANGA

NARUTO™

VOL. 15

NARUTO'S NINJA HANDBOOK!

STORY AND ART BY

MASASHI KISHIMOTO

CHARACTERS
Sasuke
サスケ
Naruto
ナルト
Guy ガイ
Sakura
サクラ
Neji ネジ
Rock Lee
ロック・リー
Tenten
テンテン
Shikamaru
シカマル
Kiba &
Akamaru
キバ&
赤丸
Hinata
ヒナタ
Gamabunta
ガマブン太
Ino いの
Choji
チョウジ
Shino シノ

The Story So Far…

Twelve years ago a destructive nine-tailed fox spirit attacked the ninja village of Konohagakure. The Hokage, or village champion, defeated the fox by sealing its soul into the body of a baby boy. Now that boy, Uzumaki Naruto, has grown up to be a ninja-in-training, learning the art of ninjutsu with his teammates Sakura and Sasuke.

Naruto and company take on the Chûnin Selection Exams but suffer a sudden attack from Orochimaru in the Forest of Death. Orochimaru leaves a curse mark on Sasuke's body and vanishes…

Then, during the finals of the Chûnin Exams, Orochimaru, disguised as Kazekage, takes the Hokage hostage and erects a barrier shield. *Operation Destroy Konoha* is under way as Naruto chases after Sasuke and Gaara, who have both disappeared.

NARUTO

VOL. 15

NARUTO'S NINJA HANDBOOK!

CONTENTS

HUF
HUF
Number 127: To Feel Alive...!!
HUF

UZUMAKI NARUTO
UCHIHA SASUKE

GAARA OF THE SAND
Number 127:
To Feel Alive...!!

NARUTO
-ナルト-

SHUDDER
...IT'S THE SAME EYE...
...AS EARLIER...!!
QUIVER
QUIVER
!!
CROUCH

RRRROAR!!
愛

KA BOOM
ROCK
SPLINTER
RRRUMBLE
BOOM

...HE... REALLY IS A MONSTER ...
HWOO HWUFFF
DO YOU FEAR ME?
UCHIHA... SASUKE!
...

READ THIS WAY

YOU'VE GOT EYES THAT KNOW REAL ISOLATION...
!!
...
...AND...
...EYES THAT RECOGNIZE IT AS THE GREATEST PAIN IN THIS WORLD...

I THOUGHT I TOLD YOU. YOU HAVE EYES LIKE MINE...
...EYES SEEKING STRENGTH, SPILLING OVER WITH HATRED AND INTENT TO KILL...
JUST LIKE ME...
...EYES ITCHING TO KILL THOSE WHO DROVE YOU INTO THE TORTURE CALLED SOLITUDE...
...
酒

THAT'S IT, THOSE ARE THE EYES...
ALL RIGHT, HOLD IT RIGHT THERE...
GAARA, RIGHT...?
!
...!
I DON'T KNOW HOW YOU THINK YOU KNOW ALL ABOUT SASUKE, BUT...
...YOU SHOULDN'T TALK LIKE YOU'VE SEEN THROUGH HIM ENTIRELY.
NOW, WHAT IN THE WORLD DID YOU WANT TO SAY TO HIM, TRACKING HIM ALL THE WAY DOWN HERE BEFORE THE FINALS?
...!
A BATTLE IS A GAMBLE ...
...WHERE ONE PITS ONE'S EXISTENCE AGAINST ANOTHER'S...

AND YOU TRY TO KILL EACH OTHER...
AND WHERE ONLY THE VICTOR GETS TO SAVOR THE WORTH OF HIS EXISTENCE.
...IN OTHER WORDS, WHAT YOU'RE SAYING IS...
"LET'S FIGHT A DEATH MATCH" AS OPPOSED TO JUST A MATCH, HMM?
UCHIHA... I KNOW... YOU ACTUALLY DESIRE IT TOO...
DEEP INSIDE YOUR HEART...
YOU WANT TO CONFIRM THE WORTH OF YOUR EXISTENCE...
YOU'RE WONDERING, "AM I REALLY AS STRONG AS I THOUGHT?"
"AM I TRULY STRONGER THAN THE OPPONENT I FACE WITH THESE HATE-FILLED EYES OF MINE?"

...
WELL, WHAT'S THE MATTER ...?!
ARE YOU AFRAID OF ME?
...
HAVE BOTH YOUR HATRED AND YOUR INTENT TO KILL... WAVERED BECAUSE OF YOUR FEAR?
IS THIS THE PITIFUL EXTENT OF YOUR EXISTENCE?
UMF

IF YOU WANT AN ANSWER...
COME ON!!
SHF
GRNCH
I WAS LEFT ALIVE...
...INTENTIONALLY... ALL BY MYSELF... FOR WHAT PURPOSE?!
!
CHIRP
CHIRP
CRACKLE
NAH... I KNOW THE REASON...
CRACKLE
CRACKLE CRACKLE
HE LEFT ME ALIVE SO HE WOULDN'T BE TORMENTED BY THE GUILT OF ANNIHI-LATING THE ENTIRE CLAN...

CHIRP CHIRP CHIRP CHIRP CHIRP
BIG BROTHER ITACHI CHOSE ME AS HIS AVENGER...
...AS THE ONE WHO WILL EVENTUALLY DESTROY HIM!

!!
RRRRRROAR
LAUNCH
LAUNCH

AAAARGH!!
...
...!!

TAP
THUMP
...?!
A-HA...
A-HA HA HA HA HA HA HA HA HA!
愛

Number 128:
Exceeding One's Limits...!!
SASUKE

A-HA
HA HA
HA HA
HA HA
HA HA!
A-HA HA HA... I SEE!
...SO THAT'S WHAT THAT WAS!
NO WAY...
SASUKE WAS ABLE TO MATCH AND COUNTER GAARA'S ENHANCED STATE ATTACK?!
...I JUST REALIZED...
WHY... I'M ENJOYING MYSELF SO!
?!
HUF
HUF
THIS PAIN...
THROB
THROB

IF I CAN DEFEAT ONE STRONG ENOUGH TO WOUND ME, ROB HIM OF ALL THAT HE IS...
HAHAHAHAHA
...I'LL FEEL EVEN MORE ALIVE THAN EVER!
...
SASUKE'S MANAGED TO WOUND GAARA TWICE NOW... GAARA, WHO HAD NEVER EVEN BEEN SCRATCHED BEFORE...
IS HE... A MONSTER TOO?
HUF
HUF
NAH... THE REAL MONSTER IS INSIDE GAARA...
BUT ONLY HIS RIGHT ARM TRANS-FORMED...

HA, HA, HA! MORE, I WANT MORE!
SLITHER SLITHER
SLITHER
ARGH!!!
!!
!!
HUF
HUF
HUF

READ THIS WAY
ONE AFTER ANOTHER ...
...WHAT IS HE?!!
READY FOR ME?!!
CLENCH
LAUNCH
HE'S EVEN FASTER THAN BEFORE!

SHAA
UGH!
SWAP
FWAM
KLAK
KLAK

STRETCH
I CAN'T EVEN DODGE HIM WITHOUT TAKING TIME TO PREDICT HIS MOVES...
WITHOUT THE SHARINGAN, I'D ALREADY BE DEAD...
WHOOM!
BUT... SINCE I ALREADY USED IT ONCE IN THE MATCH... AND AGAIN JUST NOW...
...I CAN'T USE THE CHIDORI ANYMORE...
FWIP
HUF
FIRE STYLE...

BLAZ
!!!
GÔKAKYÛ NO JUTSU! FIRE STYLE! FIREBALL TECHNIQUE!!
DIE!
SKA
RINK
...THE JUTSU JUST ISN'T POWERFUL ENOUGH...
I GUESS FIRE IS INEFFECTIVE AGAINST SAND...
I GUESS...
... CHIDORI'S MY ONLY CHOICE.
FAMP

WHAM
UGH!!
HUF
HUF
HUF
SLAM
HUF
HUF
HUF
IT LOOKS LIKE YOUR LIMIT IS TWO CHIDORI...
...AT LEAST FOR NOW.

!!
ARGH...!
CRACKLE CRACKLE FIZZ...
HUF
HUF
HUF
TWITCH
HUF
HUF
HUF
HUF
RIGHT NOW, YOU ONLY HAVE ENOUGH CHAKRA TO EMIT TWO CHIDORI A DAY.
HUF
HUF
CHIDORI...
...IS A JUTSU YOU CAN ONLY USE JOINTLY WITH THE SHARINGAN IN A BATTLE SITUATION...
AND USING SHARINGAN AND OTHER JUTSU AT THE SAME TIME...
...IS LIKE COMBUSTING AND EXPENDING ALL OF YOUR BODY'S CHAKRA AT ONCE...
...
HUF
HUF
HUF
FIZZLE FIZZLE

READ THIS WAY

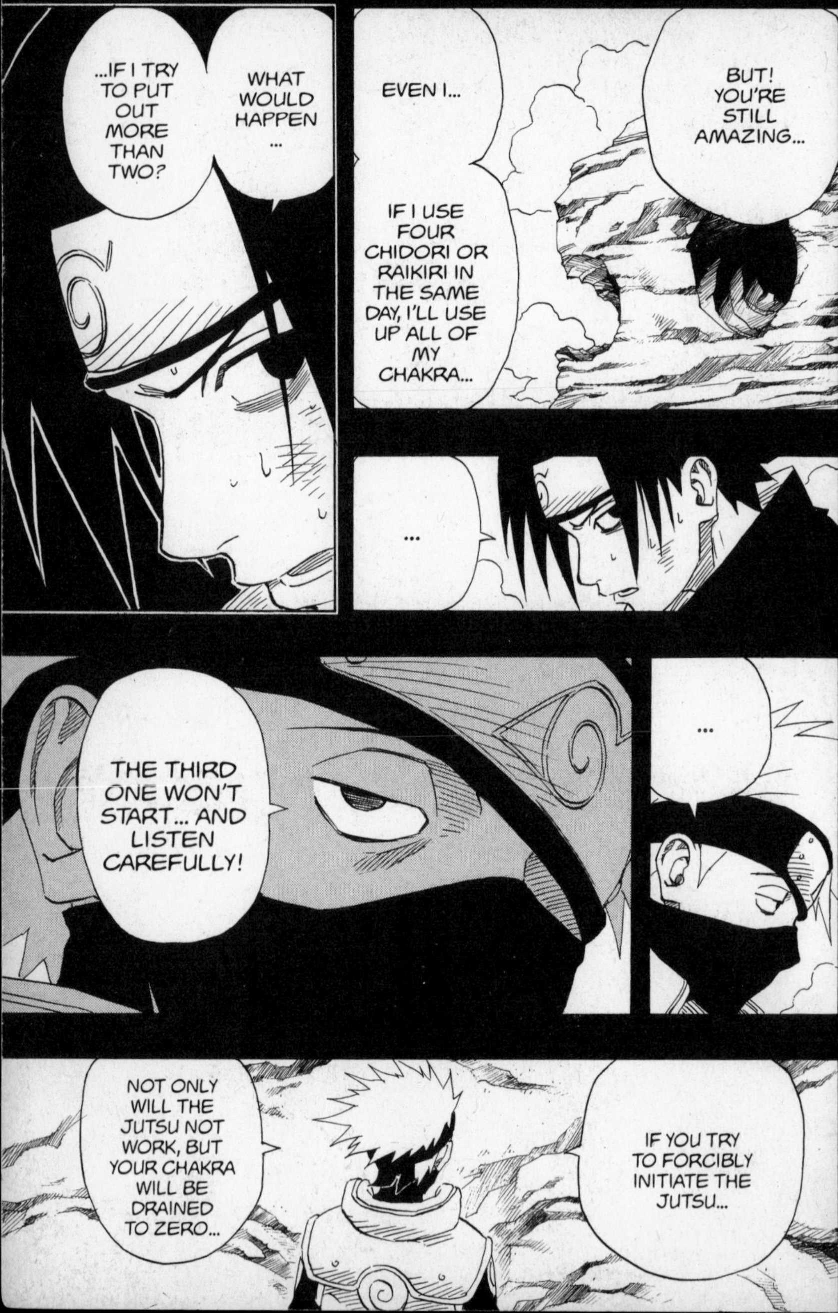

AND IF YOU'RE NOT CAREFUL, YOU'LL DIE.
EVEN IF YOU SURVIVE IT... I GUARANTEE THAT IT WON'T BE GOOD FOR YOU.
...ESPECIALLY FOR YOU...
HUF
HUF
HUF
IS THIS ALL YOUR EXISTENCE IS WORTH?
LET ME TELL YOU...
YOU'RE WEAK!!
FWUMP

READ THIS WAY

'CUZ YOU'RE NAÏVE...
AND YOUR HATRED IS NOT STRONG ENOUGH.
...
THE STRENGTH OF ONE'S HATRED IS THE STRENGTH OF ONE'S WILL TO KILL...
AND THE STRENGTH OF ONE'S WILL TO KILL IS THE STRENGTH OF VENGEANCE.
...
YOUR HATRED WILL NEVER MATCH MINE!!
SHUT UP...
DO YOU UNDER-STAND ME...?

ZAP
IT MEANS...
YOU ARE WEAKER!!
LAUNCH
!
THROB
FIZZ...

CLASH

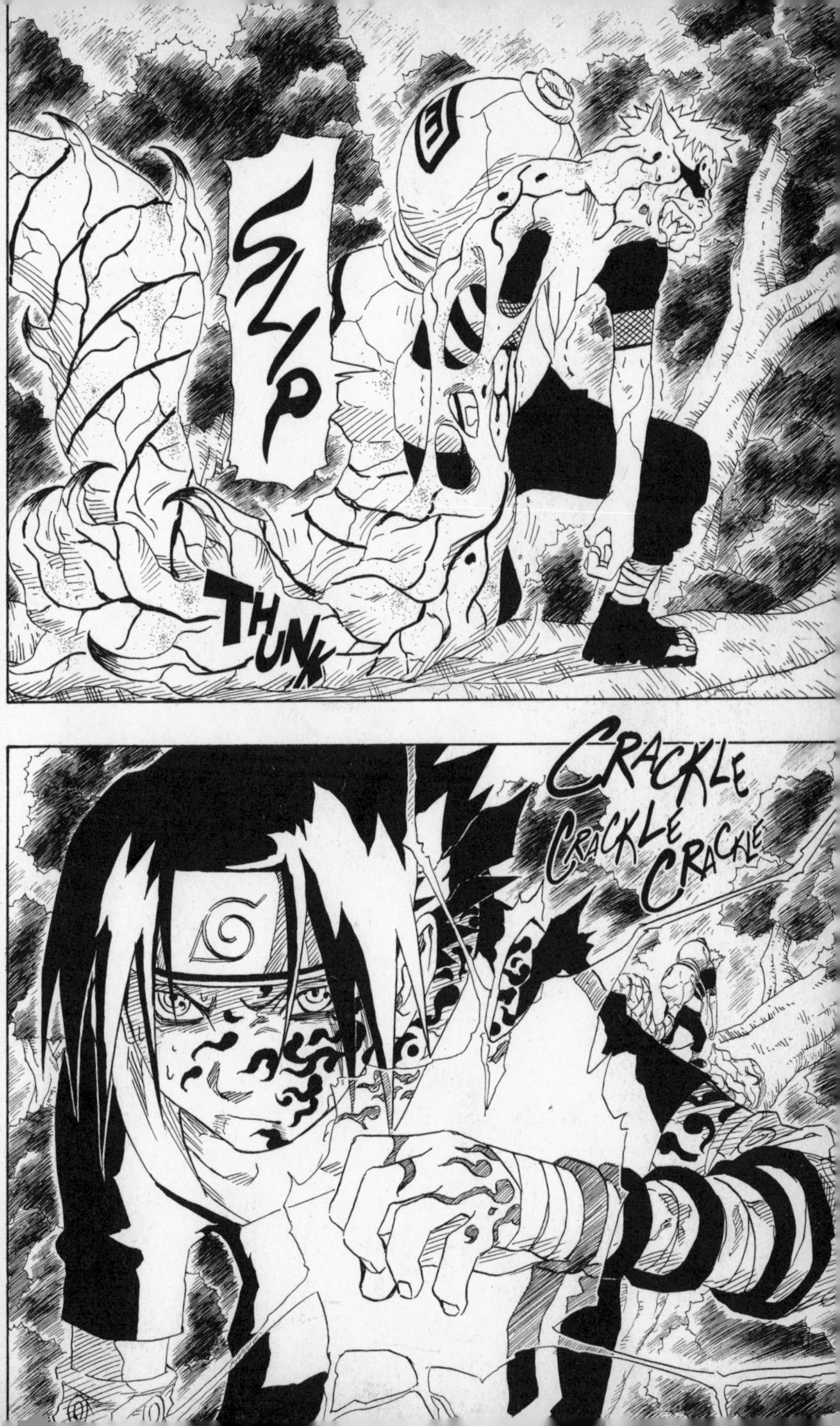
SLIP
THUNK
CRACKLE
CRACKLE CRACKLE

READ THIS WAY

KA
WHAM!
...!!!

KER THWACK
FUMP
TUMP
SASUKE!!
TAP
HUF
HUF
HUF
TMP
!

...
HUF
HUF

Number 129:
To Hurt...!!
UNH... UGH...
WE WERE ONE STEP TOO LATE.
UNH...
...THEY'RE...
UGH...
YOU ALL...

TH...
THIS IS...
HE WAS PROBABLY FIGHTING RECKLESSLY... JUST LIKE THAT TIME!!
AND MASTER KAKASHI TOLD ME I DIDN'T HAVE TO WORRY ABOUT THE MARK!
ARGGGGH...
S... SAKURA...?
SAKURA!
WHAT IS IT!!
WHO'S... THAT?!!
!
GRRRR

READ THIS WAY

I'M NOT A BATTLE TYPE NINJA DOG, SO DON'T COUNT ON ME!!
HARRUMPH!
I CAN SEE THAT!!
SO THAT'S... THAT "MONSTER," EH...
IN ANY CASE, WE'VE GOT TO GET THROUGH THIS CRISIS...
...AND SOMEHOW GET SASUKE TO MASTER KAKASHI...!!
UGH... UNNH.
...
EVEN IF YOU SURVIVE IT... I GUARANTEE THAT IT WON'T BE GOOD FOR YOU.
...ESPECIALLY FOR YOU...
...YOU MEAN THE CURSE MARK...?
UGH... UNNH...

READ THIS WAY

IF YOU GIVE IN TO HATRED AND RELY ON THE POWER OF THAT CURSE MARK...
...YOUR MATURATION WILL STOP RIGHT THERE.
AND THEN... YOU WON'T BE ABLE TO WIN AGAINST ITACHI.
HUF
HUF
...I'VE GOT TO SUPPRESS THE MARK...!
HACK!!
SASUKE!!
...

...YOU'RE... ONE... I DIDN'T GET TO KILL!
!
I WOULD FIGHT ONLY FOR MYSELF AND LOVE ONLY MYSELF.
...FOR AS LONG AS THERE ARE PEOPLE OUT THERE FOR ME TO KILL...
...THEN I WILL NOT CEASE TO EXIST.
L...LET'S RUN!!
C'MON!!
WHIRL

!
HUH?
!
DIE!
UCHIHA SASUKE!!

SHWOOSH
SAKURA!

AIEE!!
KLIP
SLAM
ARGH!!

THROB
UGH!
TAK
SWF
ZOOM
SAKURA!!
...THAT GIRL TRIED TO STAND UP TO GAARA...!

READ THIS WAY

DARN! DARN!
WHAT AM I SUPPOSED TO DO?!!
I DON'T KNOW IF I CAN HANDLE THIS GUY...
...NOW, HELP ME FEEL ALIVE.
GULP
...!

UNH...
UNH...
WHY...?

UNNH...
...
YASHAMARU...
YAH!!
KICK
THUMP
PASS!

OH--! MAN!
WHAT ARE WE GONNA DO?!
NONE OF US CAN DO THE WALL-CLIMBING TECHNIQUE...
!
SHOOO...
SHOOO
!!
Y... YOU'RE...!

READ THIS WAY

SLAM
WAAAH!
SLAM
HELP--!
I DON'T WANT TO BE ALONE ANYMORE
...
SNAP
AAAAH!
NO!
RUSH
BLOCK
UGH!!
LORD GAARA, PLEASE CALM YOURSELF!!

U...UNH...

LIFT
SLOOSH...
SLITHER SLITHER...
SLOOSH
THE SAND PROTECTS ME...
...IT'S STILL USELESS ...
LORD GAARA...
!

I MIGHT NOT LOOK LIKE IT, BUT I AM STILL A MEMBER OF THE MEDICAL CORPS CHARGED BY LORD KAZEKAGE HIMSELF TO SEE TO YOUR SAFETY AND WELL-BEING.
PLEASE DO NOT ENGAGE IN SUCH BEHAVIOR IN FRONT OF ME.
...EVEN IF THE SAND PROTECTS YOU AS WELL...
...
... YASHAMARU ...
I'M SORRY.
YOUR WOUND...
DOES IT HURT?
OH, THIS?
WELL, JUST A BIT...
BUT IT'S ONLY A SMALL SCRATCH. IT'LL HEAL IN NO TIME.
YASHAMARU ...?
HMM?
WHAT DOES IT MEAN...
TO HURT?

THE WORLD OF KISHIMOTO MASASHI
MY PERSONAL HISTORY, PART 21

IN MY SECOND YEAR OF COLLEGE, AFTER I GOT TO KNOW MY TWO MANGA-DRAWING UPPERCLASSMEN, I SELECTED THE TRADE PUBLICATIONS I WANTED TO WORK FOR, AND STARTED TO DRAW MANGA AIMED TOWARD THOSE MAGAZINES' CONTESTS.

EVEN AMONG THE NEWCOMER MANGA AWARDS, THERE'S A LOT OF VARIATION.

EACH MAGAZINE HAS A DIFFERENT STYLE OR THEME, AND IF YOU DON'T MATCH YOUR WORK TO THOSE THEMES, IT'S MORE DIFFICULT TO GET SELECTED.

FOR EXAMPLE, IF YOU DREW AND SUBMITTED A HOT-BLOODED BATTLE ACTION MANGA WITH ONLY STRAPPING MALE CHARACTERS TO A SHOJO MANGA MAGAZINE CONTEST, THE MOMENT THEY OPENED YOUR ENVELOPE AND SAW YOUR COVER ILLUSTRATION, THEY WOULD PUT IT BACK IN THE ENVELOPE, SEAL IT, AND EITHER THROW IT IN THE TRASH OR SEND IT BACK TO YOU. WELL, THAT MIGHT BE A RATHER EXTREME EXAMPLE, BUT UNLESS YOU REALLY TRY TO UNDERSTAND A MAGAZINE'S FLAVOR, YOU'LL JUST BE LABELED A "POOR MISGUIDED FOOL."

WHERE IT ESPECIALLY GETS TRICKY IS THE DIFFERENCE BETWEEN SEINEN AND SHONEN MAGAZINES. BECAUSE THEY ARE SOMEWHAT SIMILAR IN TASTES, IT'S VERY EASY TO GET THEM CONFUSED. I WAS A CASE IN POINT MYSELF. I OFTEN DREW HALF-AND-HALF MANGA THAT COULD HAVE QUALIFIED AS EITHER SEINEN OR SHONEN. THE REASON IS THAT THE MANGA THAT HAD INFLUENCED ME WERE THE SHONEN TITLE *DRAGONBALL* AND THE SEINEN TITLE *AKIRA*. THUS, I ACTUALLY WENT THROUGH A PERIOD WHERE I DEBATED WHICH FLOW I SHOULD GO WITH, AND EVEN IF I CHOSE ONE, ELEMENTS OF THE OTHER WOULD CREEP IN. BESIDES, BEYOND ANY SUPERFICIAL SIMILARITIES, THE ART DESIGN, DIALOGUE, TENSION, THEME, AND REPRESENTATION ARE QUITE DIFFERENT, SO (IN MY CASE!) I HAD TO DECIDE WHICH TYPE I WAS GOING TO DRAW AND GO WITH JUST ONE.

THUS, I MADE MY CHOICE, WHICH AT THAT TIME WAS TO AIM FOR SEINEN MAGAZINES. AT THE TIME, THE *AKIRA* INFLUENCE WAS GREATER IN MY ART STYLE AND NAME [OUTLINE/STORYBOARDS], AND I THOUGHT THAT MY PERSONALITY WAS MORE SUITED TOWARD SEINEN MAGAZINES AS WELL. HOWEVER, WHEN I TRIED TO DRAW SEINEN-AIMED MANGA, I JUST COULDN'T GET RID OF THE FEELING THAT SOMETHING WASN'T RIGHT, AND IT DIDN'T GO WELL... I REALIZED I HAD TO CONTEMPLATE WHAT I WANTED TO DRAW A LOT DEEPER, AND THE MORE I ANALYZED IT, THE "THING" THAT HAD PERMEATED THE DEPTHS OF MY HEART KEPT RISING TO THE SURFACE. IT WAS THAT INVINCIBLE MASTERPIECE OF SHONEN MANGA... *DRAGONBALL*... (AND YOU KNOW FROM *NARUTO* WHAT'S HAPPENED SINCE ☺).

Number 130: Love...!!
...WHAT DOES IT MEAN...
...TO HURT?
...I... I'VE NEVER EVEN BEEN INJURED, SO...
I WAS WONDERING WHAT IT FELT LIKE...
...
...
WELL... I'M NOT SURE HOW TO DESCRIBE IT...
IT'S KINDA PAINFUL... KINDA UNBEARABLE...
IN SHORT, I GUESS YOU COULD IMAGINE... BEING HIT OR CUT AND YOU CAN'T HOLD IT IN OR BE YOURSELF ANY LONGER...
I CAN'T REALLY DESCRIBE IT...
IT'S NO FUN, DEFINITELY...

...
YASHA-MARU...
!
...THEN...
YASHAMARU, DO YOU...
...HATE ME?
...

READ THIS WAY

HUMANS LIVE THEIR LIVES HURTING OTHERS AND BEING HURT IN RETURN.
BUT EVEN DESPITE ALL THAT...
...PEOPLE STILL LOVE MORE THAN THEY HATE...
...THANKS, YASHAMARU...
MAYBE I AM STARTING TO UNDERSTAND... WHAT IT MEANS TO HURT, NOW.
...IS THAT SO...?
...
SO... COULD I BE INJURED TOO?
JUST LIKE EVERYONE ELSE...
?!
IT... ALWAYS HURTS.
...!
...

IT DOESN'T BLEED...
BUT IT HURTS RIGHT HERE.
SKRCH
...

READ THIS WAY

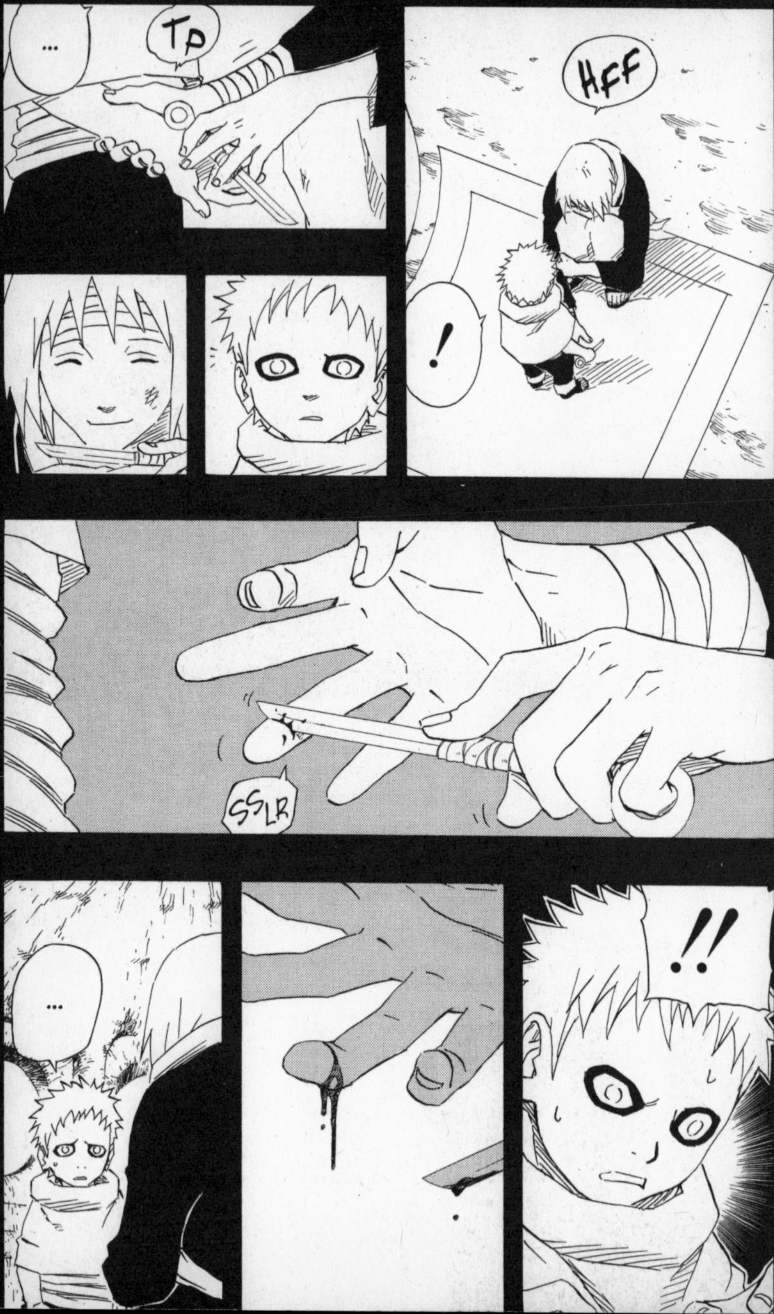

A WOUND OF THE BODY CERTAINLY BLEEDS...
AND CAN APPEAR PAINFUL.
BUT AS TIME PASSES, THE PAIN WILL FADE ON ITS OWN...
AND IF ONE USES MEDICINE, IT WILL HEAL EVEN FASTER.
...!
TAP
...BUT WHAT ARE TROUBLESOME ARE THE WOUNDS OF THE HEART...
THEY ARE EXTREMELY SLOW TO HEAL.
...WOUNDS OF THE HEART?
WOUNDS OF THE HEART ARE A BIT DIFFERENT.
UNLIKE WOUNDS OF THE BODY, THERE ARE NO MEDICINES THAT CAN HELP THEM GET BETTER...
AND SOMETIMES, THEY NEVER EVER HEAL.
...
...

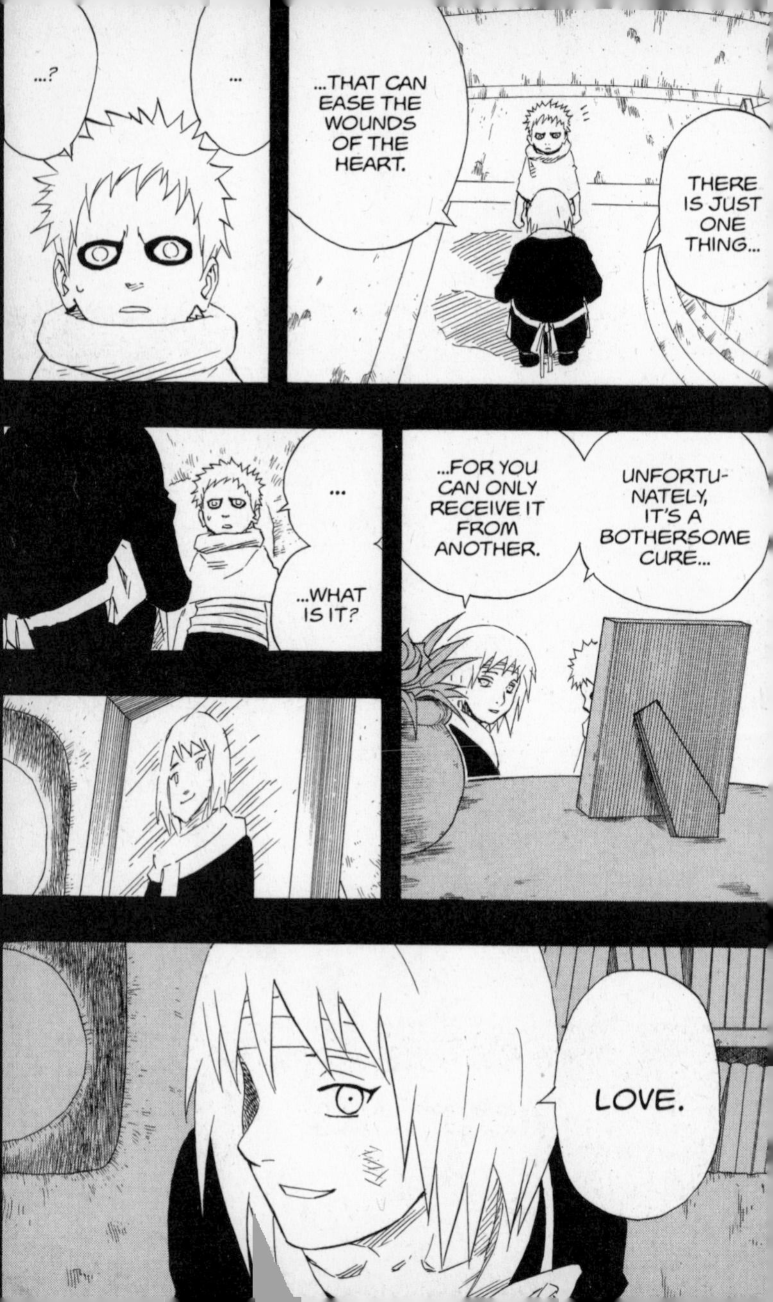
THERE IS JUST ONE THING...
...THAT CAN EASE THE WOUNDS OF THE HEART.
...
...?
UNFORTU-NATELY, IT'S A BOTHERSOME CURE...
...FOR YOU CAN ONLY RECEIVE IT FROM ANOTHER.
...
...WHAT IS IT?
LOVE.

LOVE?
YES.
...
...B...BUT, SO HOW CAN ONE RECEIVE IT?
YOU HAVE ALREADY RECEIVED SOME, LORD GAARA.
I HAVE?
LOVE IS...
...THE FEELING THAT MAKES YOU WANT TO STRIVE FOR AND PROTECT THOSE AROUND YOU WHO ARE PRECIOUS TO YOU.
...JUST LIKE ELDER SISTER...

...
I TRULY BELIEVE ELDER SISTER LOVED YOU VERY DEEPLY, LORD GAARA.
SHUKAKU OF THE SAND IS SUPPOSED TO BE A WRAITH USED FOR OFFENSIVE ASSAULTS.
WHEN THE SAND TRIES TO PROTECT YOU, I BELIEVE IT'S AN EXPRESSION OF MATERNAL LOVE.
I THINK THAT YOUR MOTHER'S WILL HAS SEEPED INTO THAT SAND.
...
ELDER SISTER...
...MUST HAVE WANTED TO PROTECT YOU...
...EVEN UNTO HER DEATH...

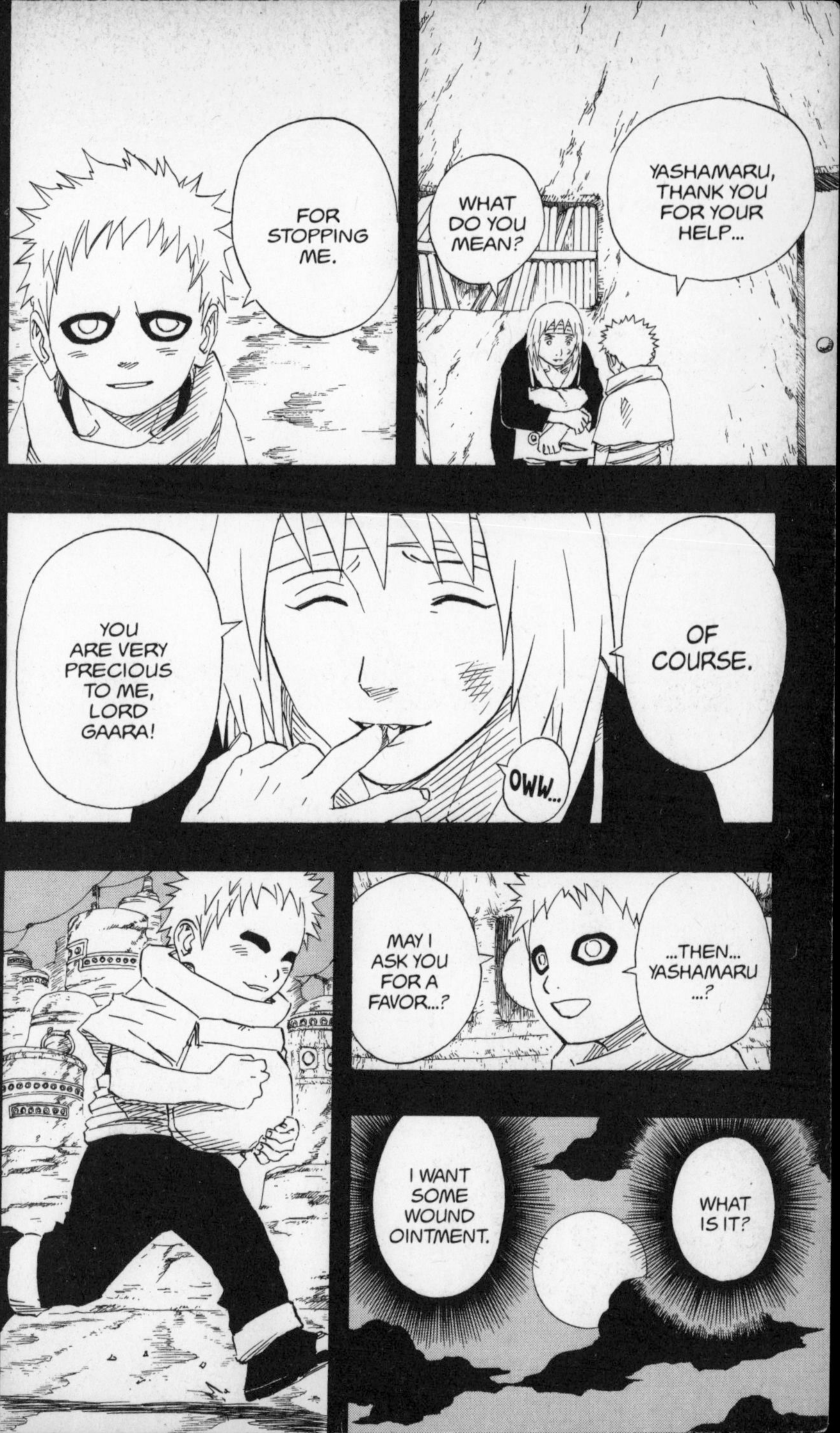
YASHAMARU, THANK YOU FOR YOUR HELP...
WHAT DO YOU MEAN?
FOR STOPPING ME.
OF COURSE.
OWW...
YOU ARE VERY PRECIOUS TO ME, LORD GAARA!
...THEN... YASHAMARU ...?
MAY I ASK YOU FOR A FAVOR...?
WHAT IS IT?
I WANT SOME WOUND OINTMENT.

KNOCK
KNOCK
CLATTER
I'M SORRY ABOUT EARLIER... IT MUST HAVE HURT...
HERE'S SOME WOUND OINTMENT, PLEASE TAKE...
...GO HOME, MONSTER...
...

HEY, WATCH WHERE YOU'RE GOING, BR...
BUMP
...UNH,
YOU'RE...
!!
THAT LOOK...
...AGAIN...!
WHY...
WHY...?!
SLITHER SLITHER
...H... HEY...!

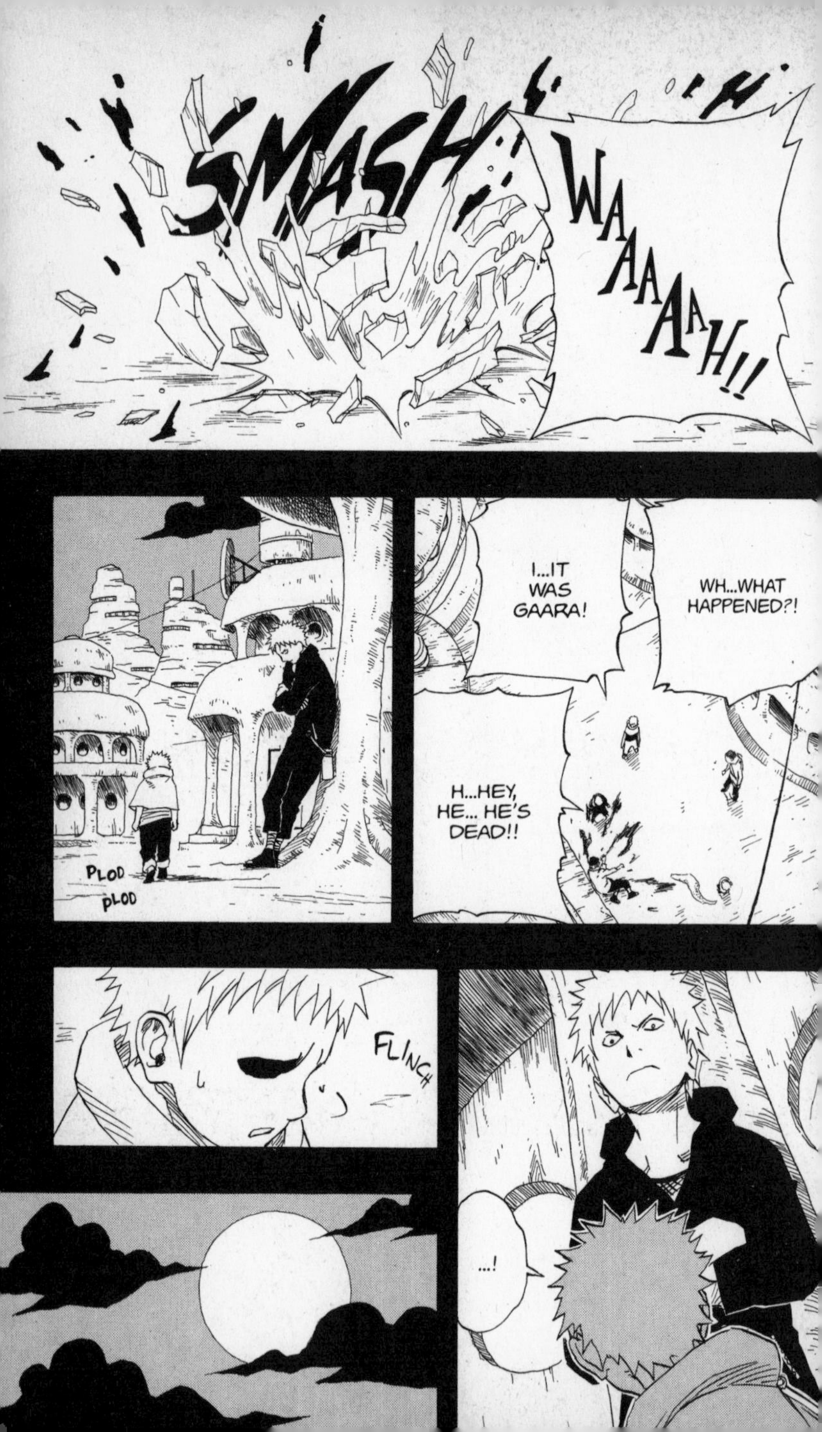
WAAAAAH!!
SMASH
WH...WHAT HAPPENED?!
I...IT WAS GAARA!
H...HEY, HE... HE'S DEAD!!
PLOD
PLOD
...!
FLINCH

IT STILL DOESN'T WORK...
I GUESS...
SKREEEE
WHY... AM I SUCH A MONSTER?!
WHAT... AM I...!?
THERE IS JUST ONE THING THAT CAN EASE THE WOUNDS OF THE HEART.
LOVE.
...
...YASHAMARU...

SHOOOM
THOCK
THOCK
THOCK
THUNK
HUH?
!!
VMMM
VMMM
VMMM
VMMM
VMMM
!!
...WHAT?!
...WHY?!
WHY ME...?!!
ALWAYS ME!!

FWSH
T-HOOM
!!
SLITHER SLITHER
THONK THONK
THOCK THOCK
CLENCH
SQUELCH

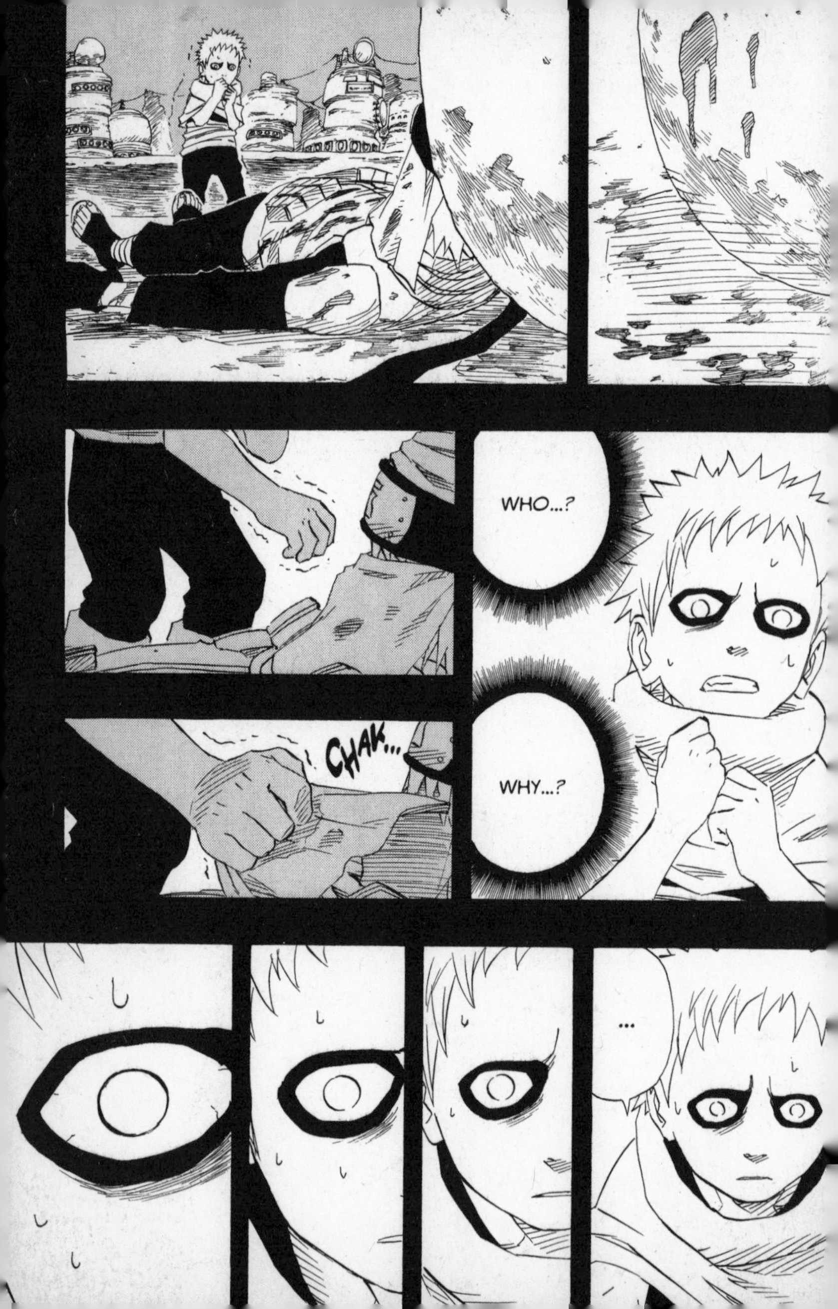
WHO...?
WHY...?
CHAK...
...

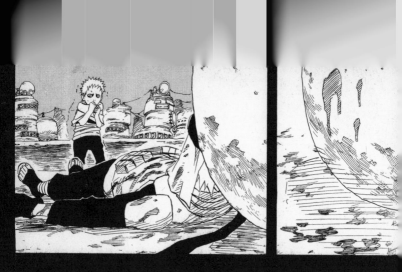

YOU TRULY ARE IMPRES- SIVE...
LORD GAARA...
...YASHAMARU...
DANG
SKRENCH

READ THIS WAY
AAAAAARGH!!

THE WORLD OF KISHIMOTO MASASHI
MY PERSONAL HISTORY, PART 22

SO AFTER ALL THAT, HAVING DECIDED I WOULD AIM FOR SHONEN MAGAZINES, I IMMEDIATELY CHOSE WITHOUT ANY HESITATION THE SPECIFIC SHONEN MAGAZINE WHOSE CONTEST I WOULD ENTER. OF COURSE, I CHOSE *WEEKLY SHONEN JUMP*, THE MAGAZINE IN SHICH *DRAGON BALL* APPEARED.

HOWEVER, I SUDDENLY RAN RIGHT INTO A WALL...

BECAUSE I HAD INITIALLY BEEN AIMING FOR SEINEN MAGAZINES, MY ART STYLE WAS NO LONGER SHONEN. WELL, TO A CERTAIN EXTENT, I COULD STILL DRAW SHONEN-LIKE STYLE, BUT I JUST COULDN'T GET CRAZY ABOUT MY CHARACTER DESIGNS. I HAD BEEN GROPING ABOUT FOR AN ORIGINAL ART STYLE THIS WHOLE TIME, BUT THERE WAS ONE OTHER THING THAT WASN'T GOING WELL AT ALL FOR ME. I COULD DRAW PLENTY OF ROUGH SKETCHES OR STORYBOARDS, BUT THEN I COULDN'T FIGURE OUT HOW TO EXPRESS THEM WELL WITH LINES; IN SHORT, HOW ONE DISTORTS AND EXPRESSES LINES REFLECTS THAT INDIVIDUAL'S SENSE.

AT THE TIME, I HAD BEEN SEARCHING HIGH AND LOW WITHOUT SUCCESS FOR NEW DRAWINGS THAT HAD GOOD SENSE IN ADDITION TO BEING GREAT ART, BUT THERE HAD BEEN NOTHING SINCE *AKIRA* THAT HAD CAUGHT MY EYE.

AND THEN ONE DAY, I SAW AN ANIME THAT TOTALLY BLEW ME AWAY... BECAUSE IT CONTAINED ALL OF THE ELEMENTS I HAD BEEN SEEKING. THAT ANIME WAS *HASHIRE MEROSU* [RUN, MELOS].

Number 131:
The Name Gaara...!!
AAAAARGH!!
AA... AH...
HACK...
THROB
AAH...
SQUEEZE
HUF
HUF
HUF

CHATTER
CHATTER
CHATTER
CHATTER
WH... WHY...
WHY...?
WHY...?!
WHY YOU... YASHAMARU...
WHY...?!

LOVE IS... THE FEELING THAT MAKES YOU WANT TO STRIVE FOR AND PROTECT THOSE AROUND YOU WHO ARE PRECIOUS TO YOU.
WHY...?
YOU ARE SOMEONE VERY PRECIOUS TO ME, LORD GAARA!
HUF
HUF
...
YOU...
YOU ALWAYS...
YOU WERE THE ONLY ONE WHO... EVER LOVED ME...
IT WAS AN ORDER.
HUF
!
I WAS COMMIS-SIONED TO KILL YOU.
...?!

BY YOUR FATHER...
LORD KAZEKAGE...
!!
FATHER DID...?
CLAP
ULP!
GAH...!!
GACK
...
HUF
HUF

WHY...
...WHY WOULD...
WHY WOULD FATHER...?
HUF
YOU, LORD GAARA... IN WHOM THE SHUKAKU WAS IMPLANTED WHILE YOU WERE STILL IN THE WOMB...
...HAD BEEN WATCHED OVER AND GUARDED UNTIL NOW AS AN EXPERIMENTAL SUBJECT.
HOWEVER, IF YOU CANNOT LEARN TO CONTROL THE SAND THAT IS THE POWER OF THE SHUKAKU WRAITH...
...YOU WILL EVENTUALLY BECOME TOO DANGEROUS FOR THE VILLAGE, LORD GAARA...
SO IT WAS DECIDED...
HUF
HUF
...
...
THEN...
...THEN YOU DIDN'T HAVE A CHOICE, YASHAMARU...
YOU HAD TO CARRY OUT FATHER'S ORDER ...

NO...
...THAT'S NOT ENTIRELY TRUE...
I CERTAINLY DID... RECEIVE AN ORDER FROM LORD KAZEKAGE.
...HOWEVER...
I PROBABLY COULD HAVE REFUSED IT IF I HAD THOUGHT TO...
!!
...!
...
BUT LORD GAARA...
DEEP DOWN INSIDE... I THINK I...

...RESENTED YOU...
...FOR STEALING THE LIFE OF MY MOST BELOVED OLDER SISTER WITH YOUR BIRTH...
...
I TRIED DESPERATELY TO LOVE YOU... EVEN IF ONLY AS A MEMENTO OF MY OLDER SISTER...
...BUT IN THE END, I COULDN'T ...
MY OLDER SISTER DID NOT WANT YOU...
SHE WAS SACRIFICED FOR THE VILLAGE AND DIED CURSING THIS PLACE...

AND SINCE THAT DAY...
I THINK I HAVE CARRIED A WOUND OF THE HEART THAT WILL NEVER HEAL...
UNLIKE WOUNDS OF THE BODY, THERE ARE NO MEDICINES THAT CAN HELP THEM GET BETTER... AND SOMETIMES, THEY NEVER EVER HEAL.
...
ELDER SISTER...
...GAVE YOU YOUR NAME, YOU KNOW.
"THIS CHILD'S NAME SHALL BE GAARA...
"A SHURA, A DEMON, WHO SHALL LOVE ONLY HIMSELF..."
"LOVE ONLY YOURSELF... AND FIGHT ONLY FOR YOURSELF...
"...SO BY DOING THAT, YOU WILL BE ABLE TO KEEP EXISTING..." THOSE WERE THE THINGS SHE WISHED FOR YOU.

HOWEVER... ELDER SISTER DID NOT NAME YOU THUS...
...BECAUSE SHE LOVED OR WORRIED ABOUT YOU...
SHE GAVE YOU THAT NAME SO THAT YOU WOULD SURVIVE AND BE A REMINDER TO THE WORLD ...
...A REMINDER OF HER HATRED, OF HOW SHE WENT TO HER DEATH LOATHING AND CURSING THE WORLD... REMIND THEM... AND SHOW THEM ALL...!
NO, YOU WERE NEVER LOVED...!
...
YANK
AND NOW...
PLEASE DIE WITH ME...

KA
BOOM
CLUNK
I TRULY BELIEVE ELDER SISTER LOVED YOU VERY DEEPLY, LORD GAARA.
...
LOVE?

READ THIS WAY
WHEN THE SAND TRIES TO PROTECT YOU, I BELIEVE IT'S AN EXPRESSION OF MATERNAL LOVE.
I THINK THAT YOUR MOTHER'S WILL HAS SEEPED INTO THAT SAND.
...UNH... ...AAH...
LOVE.
AAAAH --!!
RRRRROAR!!!

"LOVE ONLY YOURSELF...
"AND FIGHT ONLY FOR YOURSELF...!"
SO THAT'S GAARA.
ME...
I FINALLY UNDERSTAND...
I AM ALONE.
I WON'T TRUST ANYONE ELSE ANYMORE... WON'T LOVE THEM... I'M ALONE...
HEH HEH... THAT'S RIGHT...
I'M ALL ALONE...

HUF
HUF
...OH... IT'S THAT LOOK...!!
GULP
...
WHAT'S THE MATTER...?
!!
I THOUGHT YOU WERE GOING TO RUN AWAY?
...SASUKE...

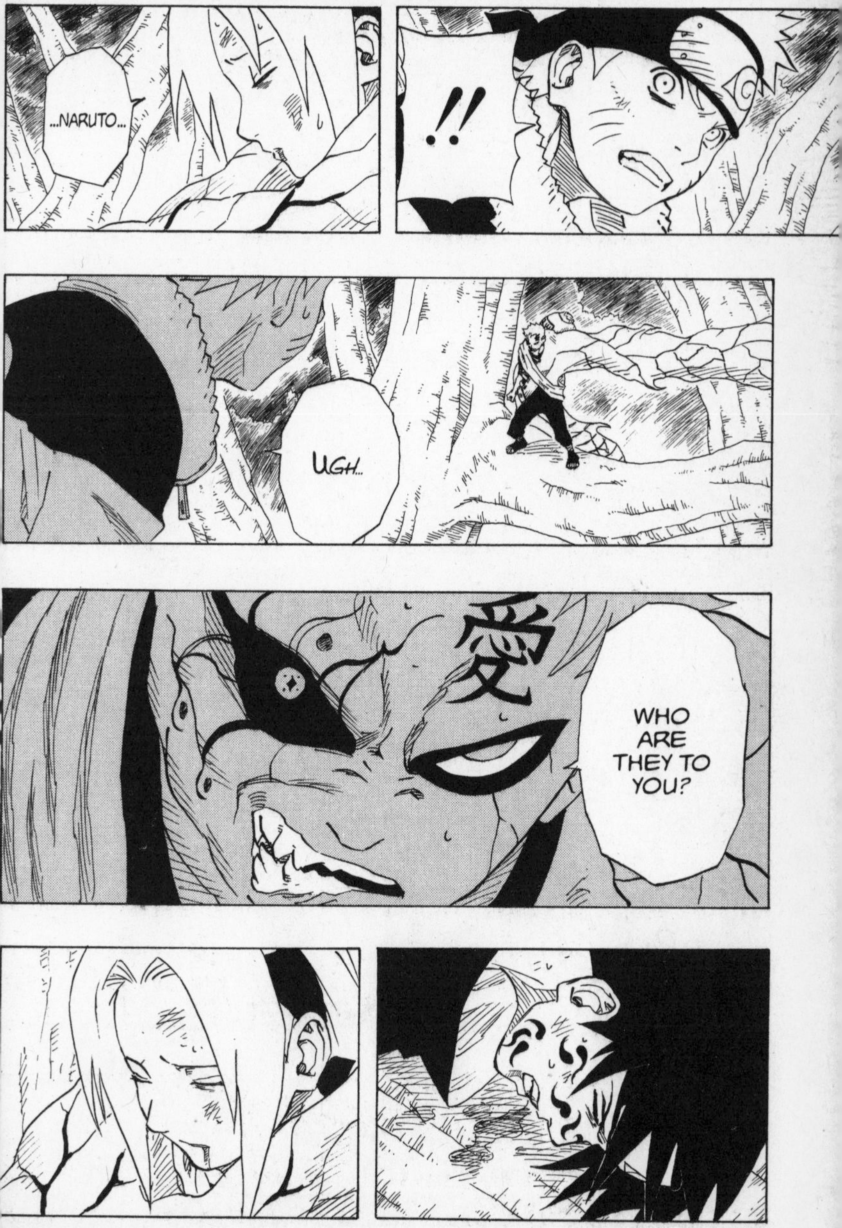
...NARUTO...
!!
UGH...
WHO ARE THEY TO YOU?

TH...THEY'RE MY FRIENDS!
IF YOU TRY TO TOUCH THEM AGAIN...
I'LL SLAUGHTER YOU!!
...
PRESS
AIEEE!!
!!
...!!
WELL... WHAT'S THE MATTER? I THOUGHT YOU WERE GOING TO SLAUGHTER ME?
UGH...
COME ON, THEN.

LEAP
DARN!
!
THWA
CK
SLAM
...!!
...DARN!

READ THIS WAY

KUCHIYOSE! SUMMONING!!
BOOF
...
WHAT THE?! YOU'RE JUST A BRAT!!
IF YOU WANT MY HELP, GIVE ME SOME MUNCHIES!
OR ELSE I WON'T PLAY WITH YOU!

READ THIS WAY
Y'KNOW, I REALLY!! I REALLY REALLY HATE YOU FROGS!!!
WHAT?! DON'T YOU DARE MOCK AMPHIBIANS!!! EH!!!
ARGH...
GRRR
FWP
THIS ISN'T THE TIME OR PLACE TO BE PLAYING AROUND, MINI-WART!
DARN! WHY IS IT...
WHAT WAS ALL THAT TRAINING FOR? AT THIS RATE, THERE ISN'T...
FRIEND...?! WHAT A LAUGH...
LOOOOM
I FIGHT...
...ONLY FOR MYSELF!!

THE WORLD OF KISHIMOTO MASASHI
MY PERSONAL HISTORY, PART 22 (CONTINUED)

HASHIRE MEROSU [RUN, MELOS] REALLY AMAZED ME! THE MUSCLES AND BONE STRUCTURE WERE REPRESENTED WITH NEW LINE TECHNIQUES, AND THE DESIGNS FELT REALLY REFRESH. NOT TO MENTION REALLY COOL. I IMMEDIATELY BECAME INTERESTED IN THE CHARACTER DESIGNER AND ANIMATION DIRECTOR OKIURA HIROYUKI, AND AS I RESEARCHED HIS FILMOGRAPHY AT THE LOCAL VIDEO RENTAL STORE, I STARTED NOTICING THAT SOME OF THE ANIMATORS' NAMES APPEARED AGAIN AND AGAIN IN MANY OTHER FILMS. "OH! THIS GUY, HE WORKED ON THIS FILM TOO. OH! THIS GUY TOO!" ...ALONG THE WAY, I GOT INTO ALL SORTS OF ANIME, AND STARTED MEMORIZING THE NAMES OF VARIOUS ANIMATION DIRECTORS AND ANIMATORS. AT THAT TIME, WHEN MANGA WERE MADE INTO ANIMATION, THE ANIME OFTEN HAD BETTER ART, SO I HAD STARTED FEELING THAT ANIMATORS WERE BETTER ARTISTS. AND THAT IS WHEN MY ENCOUNTER WITH A CERTAIN TITLE AND A CERTAIN ANIMATOR IMMENSELY INFLUENCED ME.

THAT TITLE WAS JUMP'S FAMOUS *NINKÛ*, A NINJA MANGA JUST LIKE MINE. AND THE ANIMATOR WHO INFLUENCED ME WAS NISHIO TETSUYA, THE CHARACTER DESIGNER AND ANIMATION DIRECTOR FOR THE ANIMATED VERSION.

Number 132:
The Two... Darkness and Light

RRRR RRROAR!!
RIPPLE RIPPLE
HE... TRANS-FORMED AGAIN...
SLIP
SNIP
UNLESS YOU TAKE ME DOWN, THE SAND AROUND THAT GIRL WON'T DISSOLVE.
SWIP...
IN FACT, IT WILL SLOWLY CONSTRICT, EVENTUALLY SMOTHERING AND CRUSHING HER!
愛

READ THIS WAY

VOOSH
SAND SHURIKEN!!
!
SNATCH
!!
CURL

SLAM
UGH!!
!
UGH...
...UGH, SHUT UP!
YOU'RE WEAK!
DARN!! ...WHY DID THIS MINI-TOAD SHOW UP...?!
THUD
THUD
THUMP
!
!!
BUT WHAT IN THE WORLD IS THAT THING?

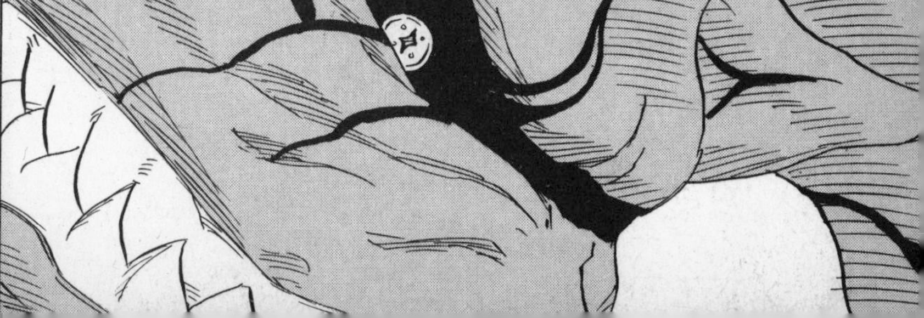

READ THIS WAY

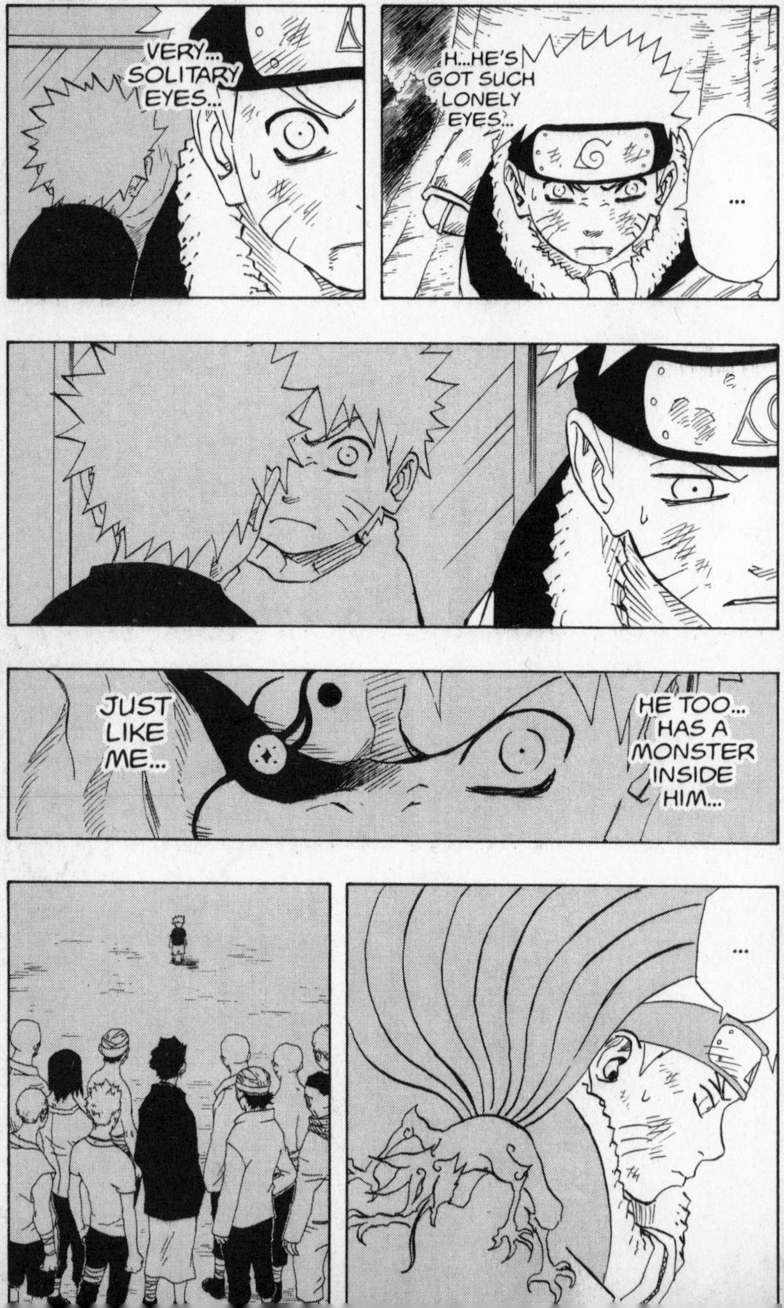
...
H...HE'S GOT SUCH LONELY EYES...
VERY... SOLITARY EYES...
HE TOO... HAS A MONSTER INSIDE HIM...
JUST LIKE ME...
...

...I DIDN'T KNOW WHO OR WHAT I WAS TO DESERVE TO BE HATED SO MUCH, OR WHY I EXISTED...
...I HATED ALL OF THEM...
IT WAS SO PAINFUL...
EVER SINCE I FOUND OUT I HAD THE NINE-TAILED FOX INSIDE ME, EVERYONE'S EYES SEEMED EVEN MORE CALLOUS...
IN OTHER WORDS, YOU...
...ARE THE NINE-TAILED FOX SPIRIT THAT DESTROYED THE VILLAGE!!
DIDN'T YOU THINK IT WAS STRANGE? TO BE SO DESPISED EVERYWHERE YOU WENT?
NARUTO! IT'S BEEN A WHILE, WANT TO GO EAT RAMEN?!
YAY! HEY! HEY! I WANT EXTRA PORK TODAY!!
...BUT...
...

HUMPH! YOU IDIOT... IF YOU WANT TO WIN AGAINST ME, TRAIN HARDER.
SHUT UP! I WON'T LOSE TO YOU!!
HEY-- NARUTO! WHAT DID SASUKE SAY ABOUT ME?
HE DIDN'T REALLY SAY ANYTHING. BUT HEY! HEY! DON'T YOU WANT TO KNOW WHAT I THINK ABOUT YOU?
HMM--... NARUTO, IF YOU KEEP EATING JUST RAMEN AND RED BEAN SOUP, YOU REALLY WILL DIE. ♡
IF YOU'RE GOING TO BE A NINJA, YOU NEED TO EAT VEGETABLES. HERE'S A DELIVERY.
Eat your veggies! Kakashi
WHAT--?! BUT I HATE VEGGIES!
I STARTED MEETING FOLK WHO WOULD ACKNOWLEDGE ME...
SO ...
EVEN THOUGH I HAD A FOX DEMON INSIDE ME, AND PEOPLE LOOKED COLDLY AT ME, I GOT USED TO IT.
CUZ...
I WASN'T ALONE ANY-MORE!!

I NEVER IMAGINED IT WOULD BE SO JOYFUL AND HAPPY...
...I AM SO... SO GRATEFUL, DEEPLY GRATEFUL...
...IT'S OKAY FOR ME TO BE ALIVE... TO EXIST.
THAT'S WHY WHEN I THINK ABOUT THE PAST, IT MAKES ME SHUDDER.
...THAT PAIN WASN'T JUST ANYTHING... IT WAS JUST PITCH BLACK.
IF... IF I HAD STAYED ALL ALONE...

CRACK
THAT'S WHY I REALLY DO UNDERSTAND IT.
TO THEM, I AM NOW A RELIC OF THE PAST THAT THEY JUST WANT TO ERASE AND FORGET.
SO FOR WHAT PURPOSE DO I EXIST, WHY AM I ALIVE?
SO THIS IS WHAT I CAME UP WITH...
"I EXIST TO KILL ALL HUMANS OTHER THAN MYSELF."

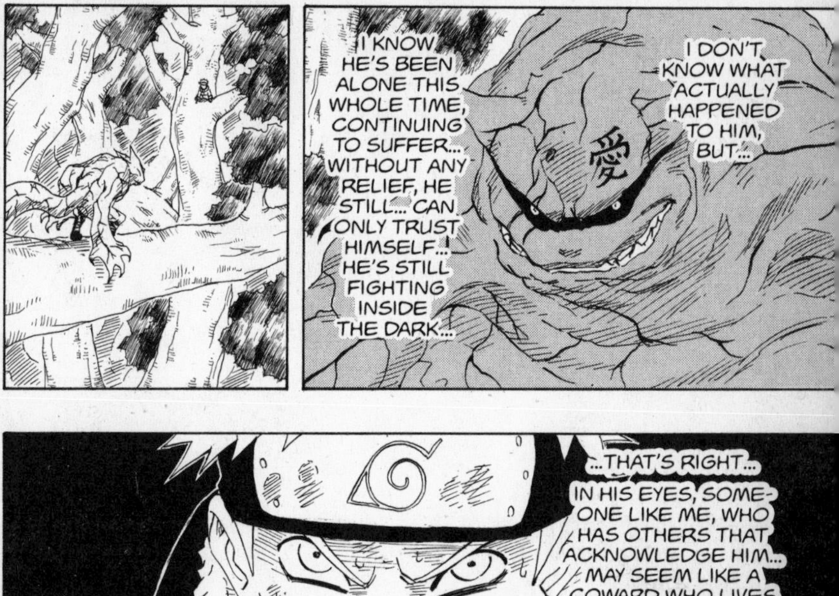
I DON'T KNOW WHAT ACTUALLY HAPPENED TO HIM, BUT...
I KNOW HE'S BEEN ALONE THIS WHOLE TIME, CONTINUING TO SUFFER... WITHOUT ANY RELIEF, HE STILL... CAN ONLY TRUST HIMSELF...! HE'S STILL FIGHTING INSIDE THE DARK...
...THAT'S RIGHT...
IN HIS EYES, SOMEONE LIKE ME, WHO HAS OTHERS THAT ACKNOWLEDGE HIM... MAY SEEM LIKE A COWARD WHO LIVES IN A CAREFREE, SUNNY WORLD...
...CAN I REALLY WIN AGAINST HIM...?
UNH...
WRRSH

READ THIS WAY

...
WELL?! WHAT'S THE MATTER!
IF YOU DON'T FIGHT ME, I'LL KILL THAT GIRL!
SLUMP
HUF
...UGH...
HUF
FSSH
DARN!
LEAP

READ THIS WAY

BOOM...
YIKES... THAT REALLY HURT...
UGH...
FIRST, I'M GOING TO PLAY WITH YOU WITHOUT LETTING YOU DIE.
I WANT TO SEE HOW LONG IT TAKES FOR YOU TO GIVE UP ON YOUR FRIENDS AND TRY TO RUN AWAY.
BUT YOU WON'T ESCAPE.
SHF
...
HUMPH...
THUD
THUD

READ THIS WAY

...
SAND SHURIKEN!!
SLASH
...ARGH...
WHY...DO I FEEL LIKE THIS...
SHF
...
GAH!!
WHOOOOOM
...!
...DARN...
...DARN...
SLUMP

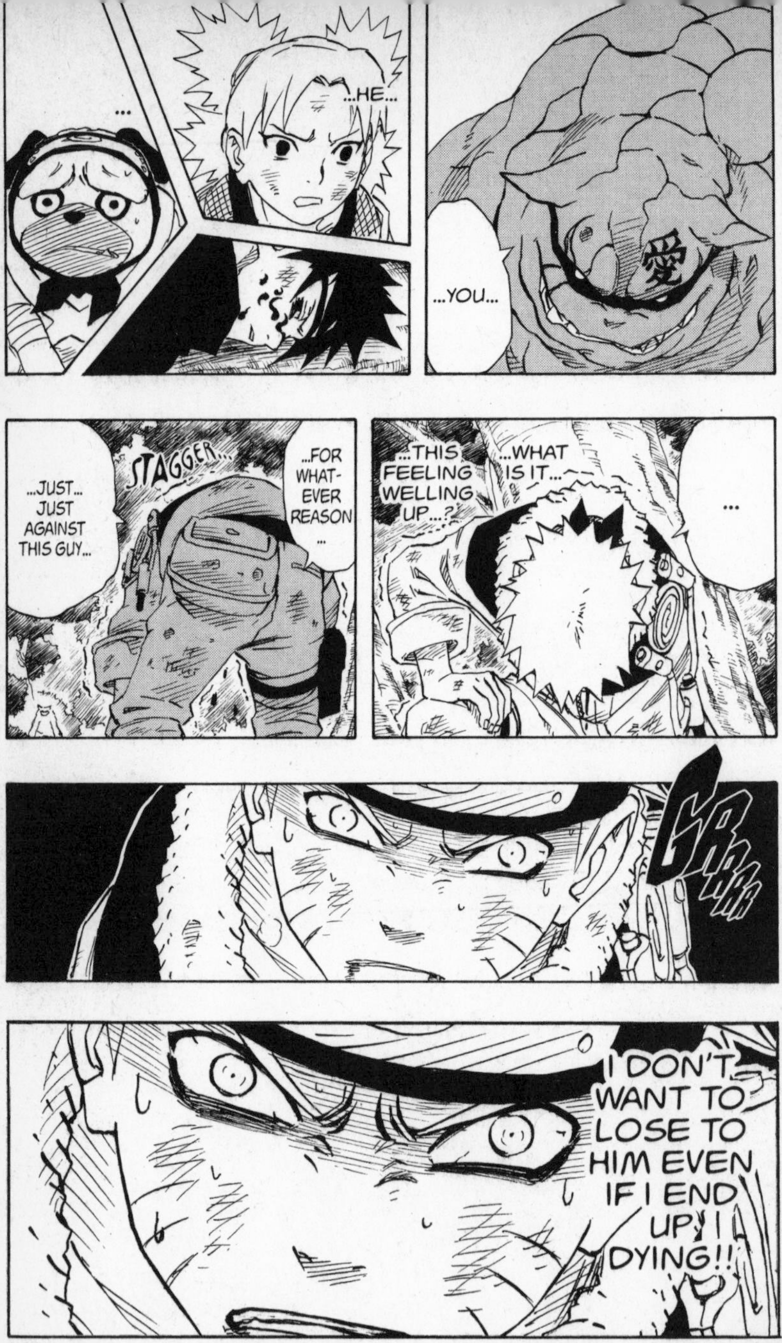
...YOU...
...HE...
...
...
...WHAT IS IT...
...THIS FEELING WELLING UP...?
...FOR WHAT-EVER REASON ...
STAGGER...
...JUST... JUST AGAINST THIS GUY...
GRAAA
I DON'T WANT TO LOSE TO HIM EVEN IF I END UP DYING!!

THE WORLD OF KISHIMOTO MASASHI
MY PERSONAL HISTORY, PART 22 (PART 3)

REGULARLY MIMICKING THE ART STYLES OF MY FAVORITE ANIMATORS AT THE TIME, SUCH AS OKIURA-SAN AND MORIMOTO KOUJI-SAN, STARTED SHIFTING MY STYLE TOWARD SEINEN MAGAZINES AND AWAY FROM SHONEN MAGAZINES AGAIN. ...THAT'S WHEN I FORTUITOUSLY SAW IN MY TARGET MAGAZINE THAT THE SERIES THAT I LIKED EVEN AS A MANGA, *NINKÛ*, HAD BECOME ANIMATED, SO I DECIDED I WOULD WATCH IT WHILE EATING A SALMON BENTO AND PREPARED MY MEAL AND SAT MYSELF DOWN IN FRONT OF THE TELEVISION. THE MOMENT I STUCK THE DISPOSABLE CHOPSTICKS IN MY MOUTH TO SPLIT THEM APART, THE *NINKÛ* ANIME STARTED, AND I GOT DRAWN RIGHT INTO THE OPENING SEQUENCE WITH THE STILL UNBROKEN CHOPSTICKS FORGOTTEN IN MY MOUTH.

IT MADE SUCH AN IMPACT ON ME! FOR IT CONTAINED NEW DISTORTIONS, HAD GREAT SENSE, EVEN BETTER ART, AND ON TOP OF IT ALL, JUST INDESCRIBABLE, REALLY REFRESHING LINE TECHNIQUE THAT SEEMED LIKE A MIX OF SEINEN AND SHONEN STYLES. IN SHORT, IT WAS THE IDEAL ART STYLE THAT I HAD BEEN SEEKING.

"THIS IS IT!" I THOUGHT TO MYSELF.

SINCE THEN, I STARTED MIMICKING NISHIO-SAN'S DRAWINGS, AND IT PRETTY MUCH WAS THE BASIS FOR THE ART STYLE OF THIS CURRENT *NARUTO*. AND AS SOME OF YOU MAY KNOW, AMONG ONE OF THE CHARACTER DESIGNERS FOR THE *NARUTO* ANIME IS NISHIO TETSUYA-SAN HIMSELF. I AM A LUCKY MAN. THE MAN THAT I RESPECTED AND RECEIVED SO MUCH INFLUENCE FROM IS DOING DESIGNS FOR ME! IT WAS A REALLY HAPPY MOMENT FOR ME WHEN I HEARD THIS, LIKE ONE OF MY DREAMS HAD COME TRUE (AND IN THAT INSTANT, I INVOLUNTARILY PUMPED MY FISTS IN THE AIR.) PLUS, ANOTHER ONE OF THE CHARACTER DESIGNERS IS SUZUKI HIROFUMI-SAN. HE IS AN AWESOME FELLOW WHO HAS WORKED ON SOME OF MY FAVORITE ANIME. THEY ARE SUCH GREAT ARTISTS THAT I'M EMBARRASSED THAT THEY LOOK AT MY MANGA.

Number 133:
HUF
HUF
HUF
HUF
HUF
TREMBLE...
Those Who Are Strong...!!

THE LOOK IN HIS EYES... DID IT CHANGE?!
愛

SAKURA...
UNH...
SQUEEZE...
FWUP
FOLD
WHAT'S THE MATTER...? YOU'RE THE ONE WHO HUNTED ME DOWN. SCARED?
YOU CAN'T EVEN COME CLOSE TO TOUCHING ME...
WHAT A JOKE...!

I'M GONNA GIVE IT EVERY-THING I'VE GOT!!
FWUP
FWUP
!
...I DON'T KNOW HOW FAR I CAN GO OR HOW MUCH I CAN DO, BUT...
SHOMP
BOOF BOOF BOOF BOOF
ART OF THE SHADOW DOPPEL-GANGER!!!
FOOM FOOM
LADIES AND GENTS, WE NOW PROUDLY BRING YOU A MOST SECRET AND SPECIAL TECHNIQUE!! THE UZUMAKI NARUTO...
HERE WE COME!!
FWOOM FWOOM

BUNSHIN TAIATARI! DOPPEL-GANGER BODY SLAM!!
KRSH
SWOOSH

NOW!!
ROGER!!
CLENCH
CLENCH
GO!!!!
SHMP
ZOOM
HA!!
FWUP

GRAB
BOOF
SPIN SPIN
SPIN
KAGEBUNSHIN NO JUTSU! ART OF THE SHADOW DOPPEL-GANGER!!
!
ONE MORE! ART OF THE SHADOW DOPPEL-GANGER!!
BOOF
ZOOM

UGH!
TAKE THIS!!
MASTER KAKASHI'S SPECIALTY... KONOHAGAKURE VILLAGE'S MOST SACRED TECHNIQUE!!
ONE THOUSAND YEARS OF DEATH!!
POKE
...
...

WHAM
!
SIZZLE
SIZZLE
KABOOM
...KABOOM.

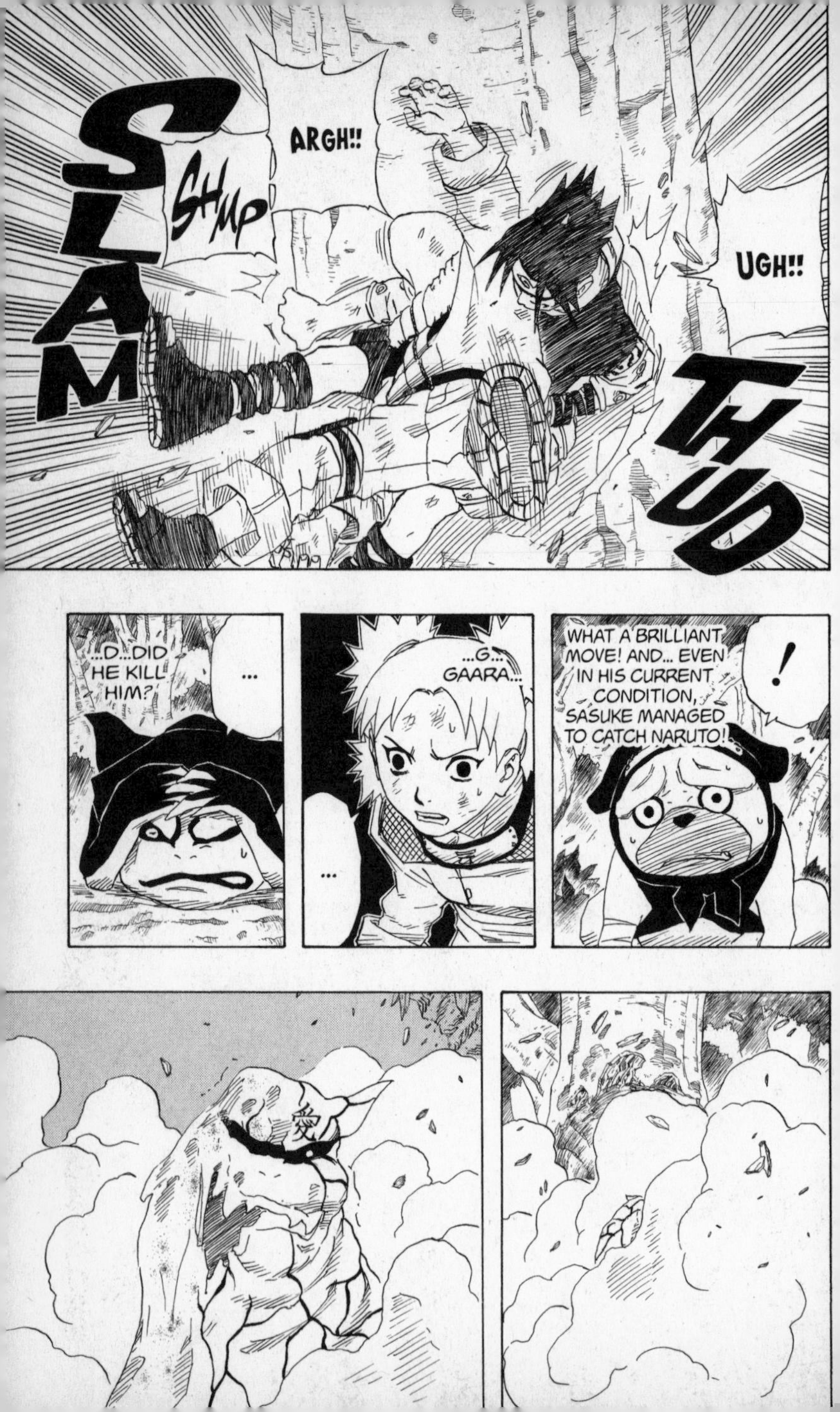
UGH!!
THUD
ARGH!!
SHMP
SLAM
!
WHAT A BRILLIANT MOVE! AND... EVEN IN HIS CURRENT CONDITION, SASUKE MANAGED TO CATCH NARUTO!
...G... GAARA...
...
...
...D...DID HE KILL HIM?
愛

...
SASUKE
...!
(HUF)
(HUF)
...BUT AFTER ALL THAT... JUST ONE BLOW?
HEH... YOU'RE FINALLY SHOWING YOUR STUFF...
(HUF)
(HUF)
SH...SHUT UP...
...IDIOT.
...YOU GOTTA TRY HARDER... 'CUZ THIS TIME... I CAN'T HELP YOU... LIKE I DID IN THE LAND OF WAVES...
...UGH... HE MANAGED TO TARGET THAT LETTER BOMB RIGHT AT MY WEAKEST SPOT—UNDER MY TAIL...
GRRR...
I CAN'T ABSORB ALL OF THE IMPACT...
I'M ENDING THIS NOW...
(HUF)
...I UNDERESTIMATED HIM... ...BUT STILL... EITHER WAY...
愛

READ THIS WAY

...HEY... NARUTO.
...!
HUF
HUF
YOU...
...BETTER RESCUE SAKURA, NO MATTER WHAT!
HUF
HUF
...!!
U... UNH.
...I TRUST YOU TO BE ABLE TO DO IT...
!!
...AND THEN... ONCE YOU FREE HER...
TAKE HER... AND GET THE HECK OUT OF HERE...
... SASUKE... WHAT...?
...EVEN IN THIS STATE... I CAN AT LEAST... DELAY HIM A LITTLE...
IT'S OVER. THAT'S ALL I CAN DO.
STRUGGLE...
STRUGGLE...
...
...NO MORE ...

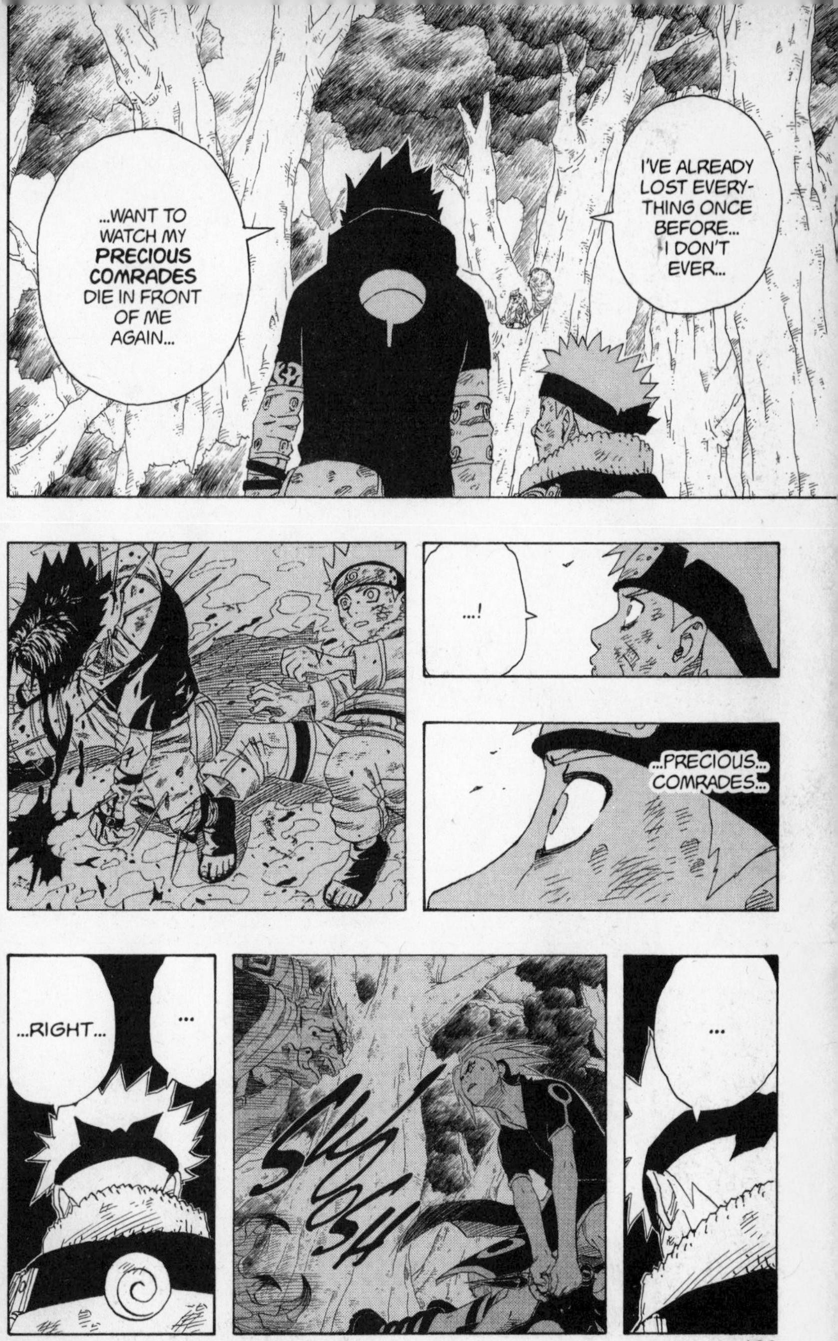
I'VE ALREADY LOST EVERY-THING ONCE BEFORE... I DON'T EVER...
...WANT TO WATCH MY PRECIOUS COMRADES DIE IN FRONT OF ME AGAIN...
...!
...PRECIOUS... COMRADES...
...
...
...RIGHT...

I WILL NEVER LET MY COMRADES DIE!
...
YOU'RE ABSO-LUTELY RIGHT...
!
...I THOUGHT OF HIM AS STRONG...
'CUZ LIKE ME, HE GREW UP WRAPPED IN LONELINESS AND SADNESS...
...AND YET HE KEPT FIGHTING FOR HIMSELF FROM INSIDE THAT CORE OF SOLITUDE...
RISE
!
HUF
HUF
... NARUTO ...
...BUT THAT'S NOT WHAT IT TAKES TO BE TRULY STRONG, IS IT...
YOU CAN'T REALLY GET STRONG JUST FIGHTING ONLY FOR YOURSELF...

...DO YOU HAVE...
...ANYONE SPECIAL IN YOUR LIFE?
WHEN PEOPLE... ARE PROTECTING SOMEONE TRULY PRECIOUS TO THEM...
...
CROUCH
...THEY TRULY CAN BECOME AS STRONG AS THEY MUST BE!
... NARUTO ...
!
愛

YOU WILL GET STRONGER...
FSSH
HAAAAAA!
AAAAAAAH!!
SHK
UNH...?!
ZAP ZAP
WH...WHOA, HE'S SUMMONING UNBELIEVABLE AMOUNTS OF CHAKRA... IS...IS THIS REALLY...
NARUTO?!
I SWEAR, I'LL PROTECT ALL OF YOU!!

TAJÛ KAGE-BUNSHIN NO JUTSU! ART OF THE MULTIPLE SHADOW DOPPELGANGERS!!!
HE'S GOOD!
!!
!
!
!!

BO
SORRY FOR THE WAIT, FOLKS!!
WE NOW BRING YOU NARUTO'S WHIRLING SWIRLING NINJA HANDBOOK!!

Number 134:
Naruto's Ninja Handbook!!

WH...WHAT THE... HOW MANY DOPPEL-GANGERS DID HE CREATE ...?!
WH... WHAT IS THIS?!
...WH...WHOA... INCREDIBLE ...
...
YOU... THIS...

SASUKE, RELAX.
LEAVE THE REST TO ME!
THIS...
...
HUF
HUF
HUF
ALL RIGHT, Y'ALL!!
TIME TO MOVE!!
GO!!
SHAA
!!
THIS IS NARUTO?!

NARUTO'S NINJA HAND-BOOK!
!!
I HAVEN'T RECOVERED FROM THAT LAST ATTACK...
I CAN ONLY SHIELD MYSELF WITH THE SAND!!
WHIP
KLAK
EVERY-WHERE SHURIKEN!!
ZAK
KLAK

CHUNK
SHOOF
SHOOF
SHOOF
THOCK
THOCK
!!
THOCK
THOCK
THOCK
THOCK
THOCK
THOCK
U!
ZU!
MA!
KI!

NARUTO'S 2000 BLOWS...

READ THIS WAY
!
愛
... BARRAGE !!

THUD
SLAM
UGH... WH...WHAT IS HE...
ALL OF A SUDDEN ...
YEAH!!
IT AIN'T OVER YET! THERE'S MUCH MORE TO COME!!
THIS TIME, WE'RE USING BOTH FEET AS WELL... A 4000 BLOWS BARRAGE!!
NO WAY... HE'S REALLY GOT GAARA CORNERED...
THERE'S NO WAY... I...I CAN'T...

I WILL NOT LOSE TO SOME-ONE LIKE YOU!
ROOOOOOAR!!
O...OH NO, DON'T TELL ME... IT'S FINALLY HAPPENING?!
POP POP POP POP
KA BOOM

SHUDDER
WH...WHAT IS THAT...?
...!
CROAK!
HIS OPPONENT IS QUITE GOOD!
IT...IT'S FINALLY EMERGED?
PERFECT POSSESSION!!
HUF
HUF
HUF
HUF
SO THAT'S... THE MONSTER THAT'S INSIDE HIM, HUH...
IT'S HUGE...

SWISH
SNAP SNAP
!!
SWIRL
HUF
HUF
WAAAAH!!
SQSH
SLITHER SLITHER
SLITHER SLITHER
DARN IT... I USED UP MY CHAKRA WITH THOSE DOPPEL-GANGERS JUST NOW...
!
NARUTO!!
!!

...
SLITHER
SLITHER
CRUNCH
SLITHER
SLITHER
SLITHER
亥 BOAR 戌 DOG
酉 ROOSTER 申 MONKEY
未 SHEEP ...
DARN! CAN'T GET UP...!!
THROB
CREAK
THROB
I CAN'T BELIEVE I WAS FORCED TO REVEAL MYSELF... BUT IT'S ALL OVER NOW...
SABAKUKYÛ! THE COFFIN OF CRUSHING SAND!

SABAKU-SÔSÔ! IMPLODING SAND FUNERAL!
POP
KUCHIYOSE NO JUTSU! THE ART OF SUMMONING!!

WHF

WHAT THE-? YOU AGAIN...?
WHAT IS IT THIS TIME?!
THE TRAINING'S FINALLY PAYING OFF! AWESOME! I CAN DO IT!!
PUMP
I SWEAR... TO PROTECT SAKURA!!
HUF
...!
OH MY...
HEY, CHIEF TOAD, SIR! FIGHT WITH ME, PLEASE, WILL YA?!!
I'M REALLY COUNTING ON YA, CHIEF!!
UZUMAKI NARUTO... WHAT... THE HECK IS HE...
HEH HEH... HE'S AN ENDLESS SOURCE OF ENTER-TAINMENT...
IF I'M NOT MISTAKEN... THAT'S SHUKAKU, THE SAND SPIRIT...
HUF

...NO THANKS!!
SHIVER SHIVER
...
...NARUTO... WHAT... HAVE YOU BEEN UP TO...
I THOUGHT YOU SAID YOU WERE GONNA MAKE ME YOUR HENCHMAN!!
RAGE RAGE
WHAT DO YOU MEAN!!
WHAT ?!!
AND WHY SHOULD I GO OUT OF MY WAY TO FIGHT THAT CREATURE...? HOW IDIOTIC.
INDEED, I DID SAY I WOULD MAKE YOU MY HENCHMAN... BUT I HAVEN'T EVEN EXCHANGED SAKÉ CUPS WITH YOU YET...
THAT'S CALLED HONOR-BOUND DUTY!!
AND A BOSS HELPS HIS HENCHMEN WHEN THEY'RE IN TROUBLE, RIGHT!
WHAP
WHAP

HOP
HOP
YOU GOT TO BE KIDDING! I'M STILL A KID!
I CAN'T DRINK!!
SQUISH
!
DON'T BE SO STUBBORN, AND HELP THIS KID, WILL YA!
AFTER ALL, HE PROTECTED ME!
PA!!
EH?!
PA?!
WHAT IN THE WORLD ARE YOU DOING HERE...
... GAMA-KICHI?!
I HAD NOTHING BETTER TO DO, SO I CAME OUT TO HAVE SOME FUN.
BUT HIM OVER THERE, HE TRIED TO BULLY ME!

WHAT~~?!
GLARE
CLICK
...KID... I'LL ACKNOWLEDGE YOU AS MY HENCHMAN!
AND I'LL SHOW YOU PLENTY OF HONOR-BOUND DUTY!!
EH? HUH? HE'S REALLY YOUR DAD?
YUP!
...
SLOOSH
I'M GOING TO SETTLE THIS SCORE... YOU LACKEY!

HE'S GOOD!

Number 135:
The Gate-Like Battle...!!

STOMP
!
ZOOM
HOLD ON TIGHT!
SWAY
WHOA!

KRAK
!
GAMA DOSUZAN! TOAD SLASH!!

SHWOOOM
WHAT A TOUGH FELLOW... HE'S SO SOLID I BARELY MANAGED TO PULL OUT THE SLASH...!
W... WOW...
CRASH
BOUNCE

SLAM
SSSHH
THUD
GAH!
WAAH!!
WHOA!

...
IF I DON'T GET RID OF HIM QUICKLY, THE WHOLE LAND-SCAPE'S GOING TO CHANGE...
HEY, CHIEF!
SAKURA'S OVER IN THAT DIRECTION, SO WE CAN'T GO THAT WAY!! CAN YOU LURE HIM OVER HERE?!!
...
SAKURA?
SHE'S HIS GIRL...
...PA.
WE'VE GOT TO TAKE HIM DOWN!
OTHERWISE, WE CAN'T SAVE SAKURA!
...

UZUMAKI NARUTO!!
FASCINATING! THIS IS GETTING FUN!!
HUH...
TH... THAT'S...!
...!
SHF
CRRK

...SO THAT'S THE HOST, HUH...
!!
SH...SHOOT, GAARA'S PLANNING TO GO ALL THE WAY...! I'VE GOT TO GET OUT OF HERE...!!
KSSSSH
IN GRATITUDE FOR GIVING ME SUCH A GOOD TIME SO FAR...
...I'LL SHOW YOU THE TRUE STRENGTH OF THE SAND SPIRIT.
...

...OUT OF FEAR!
THOSE WHO BECOME POSSESSED BY THE DEMON SHUKAKU STOP BEING ABLE TO TRULY SLEEP SOUNDLY...
LOOK AT THOSE RINGS AROUND HIS EYES.
THAT POOR HOST, HE'S GOT CHRONIC INSOMNIA FROM BEING POSSESSED BY SHUKAKU ...
?!
INSOMNIA?!
BECAUSE THEY ARE SO CHRONICALLY SLEEP-DEPRIVED, THE HOST PERSONALITY TENDS TO BECOME UN-STABLE AFTER A WHILE...!!
IF THEY WERE EVER TO TOTALLY FALL ASLEEP, SHUKAKU WOULD GRADUALLY DEVOUR THEIR PERSONALITY UNTIL THEY EVENTUALLY STOPPED BEING THEMSELVES!!
NORMALLY... WHILE THE HOST IS AWAKE...
... SHUKAKU'S TRUE STRENGTH IS SUP-PRESSED... BUT...
IF THE HOST VOLUNTARILY ENTERS SLEEP...
...

FSSS
SSF
TANUKI NEIRI NO JUTSU! THE ART OF PLAYING POSSUM !!
SLUMP
SWAY SWAY
WHA-HAHA-HAHA-HAA!!
FREE, I'M FINALLY FREE!!
!
YEAH!
OOH, STRAIGHT OUT THE GATE, I SEE SOMEONE I WANNA SLAUGHTER !!
WIND STYLE...!
FWUMP

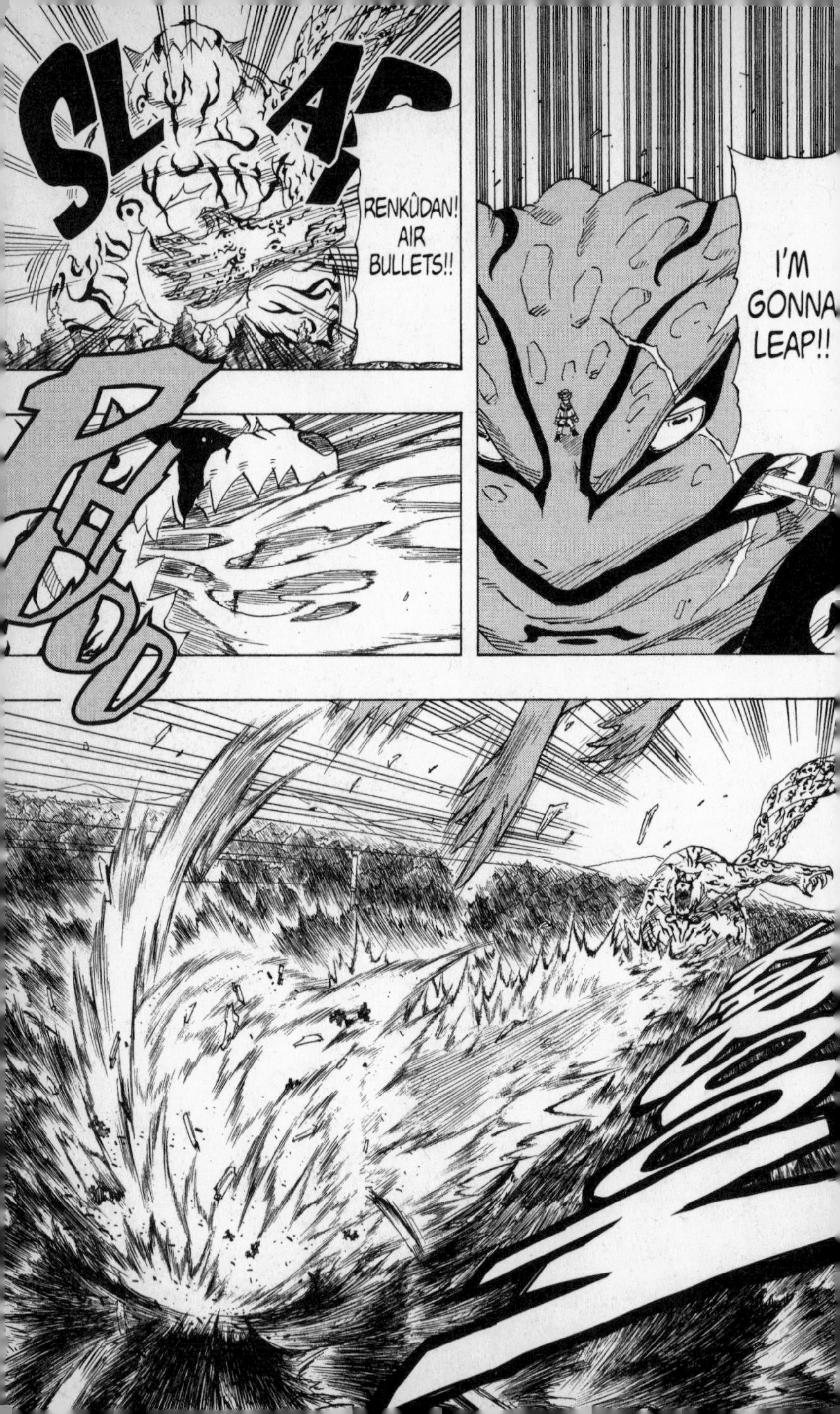
I'M GONNA LEAP!!
SLAP
RENKÛDAN! AIR BULLETS!!
PAHDD

SKOOSH
WATER STYLE...!
SKOOSH
WAAH!
LIQUID BULLETS!!
THOOT THOOT
WOOOM
AIR BULLETS!!

SHA-WOOM
PLOOSH
THIS IS LIKE A HURRICANE...
WHAT A BATTLE...
PLOOSH
WATCH OUT, CHIEF!!
THERE'S STILL ONE LEFT!
UGH!!

KA-BOOM
CRASH
WHEE! I DID IT!
I KILLED 'EM, I KILLED 'EM!!
WHOMP
!
OWW, THAT HURT! THAT LITTLE BALL WAS PACKED WITH AN UNBELIEVABLE AMOUNT OF CHAKRA!!

EVEN SOMEONE LIKE ME CAN'T TAKE MANY MORE OF THOSE LITTLE BALLS!
SO WHAT ARE WE GONNA DO?!!
THE MOST IMPORTANT THING THERE IS! WE'VE GOT TO CLOBBER THAT HOST BRAT AWAKE!!
THEN THE JUTSU WILL COME UNDONE!!
FWIP
HOW?!
WE NEED TO GET UP CLOSE AND STOP THAT FOOL'S MOVEMENTS!
THAT'LL GIVE US THE OPENING TO STRIKE!!
AGAIN, HOW?!
I'M A TOAD, I DON'T HAVE THE FANGS OR CLAWS TO HOLD HIM STILL!!
SO I'M GOING TO USE THE ART OF TRANS-FORMATION TO MORPH INTO SOMETHING PREDATORY!!

GRRR...!
TRANSFORMATION ISN'T MY STRONG SUIT!
I NEED YOU TO WEAVE THE SIGNS FOR ME... AND I'LL LEND YOU MY CHAKRA!!
IT'LL BE A COMBO TRANSFORMATION!!
'CUZ YOU USED UP THE LAST OF YOUR CHAKRA TO SUMMON ME, RIGHT?!!
SHF

EH?!! SOMETHING WITH FANGS AND CLAWS...
UHH! UHH!
HERE WE GO!!
WAIT! OH, NO!
BOOF
GRRAR

SLAM
GRAB
CHOMP
GRRRR!!
A FOX?!

TO BE CONTINUED IN NARUTO VOL. 16!

IN THE NEXT VOLUME...

EULOGY

Death in the village! When the dust settles from Orochimaru's attack, the shinobi find that not everyone has survived. While the ninja mourn, an unlikely candidate is chosen for greatness, a long-lost ninja returns with a dangerous entourage, and Naruto finds his life in more danger than ever before.

AVAILABLE SEPTEMBER 2007!

Read it first in SHONEN JUMP magazine!

GET READY FOR NINJA FEVER

MORE NARUTO THAN EVER BEFORE!

You've already caught Ninja Fever! 'Cause it starts right here!

Your ninja skills may already be sharp enough for you to have noticed that this volume of *Naruto* came out a little faster than you expected. In fact, you were able to buy it *two months* earlier than usual. That's because we've got all kinds of exciting things lined up for you in 2008! And to prepare, you need to read all the *Naruto* you can so you'll be ready for it when all the changes happen!

So instead of waiting four or five months for the next volume, you'll be able to buy twelve volumes by the end of the year. That's three volumes of *Naruto* for you to read each month for the next four months!

Are you ready to catch Ninja Fever?

Joel Enos
Editor, *Naruto*

The Naruto Schedule:

Available September 4, 2007
Naruto 16
Naruto 17
Naruto 18

Available October 7, 2007
Naruto 19
Naruto 20
Naruto 21

Available November 4, 2007
Naruto 22
Naruto 23
Naruto 24

Available December 2, 2007
Naruto 25
Naruto 26
Naruto 27

SJ
テニスの王子様
THE PRINCE OF TENNIS™
Action! Intrigue! Espionage! High School tennis has never been this exciting
$7.95
SHONEN JUMP GRAPHIC NOVEL
Story & Art by
Takeshi Konomi
THE PRINCE OF TENNIS
volume 1
Manga on sale now!
SHONEN JUMP MANGA
THE PRINCE OF TENNIS © 1999 by Takeshi Konomi/SHUEISH
On sale at:
www.shonenjump.com
Also available at your local bookstore and comic store.
RATED A FOR ALL AGES
VIZ media
www.viz.c

HOSHIN ENGI™
SJ
$7.99
HOSHIN ENGI
SHONEN JUMP MANGA
Story & Art by
Ryu Fujisaki
volume 1
MANGA
ON SALE NOW!
WHO IS BEHIND THE
MYSTERIOUS HOSHIN
PROJECT?
SHONEN JUMP
MANGA
On sale at:
www.shonenjump.com
Also available at your local
bookstore and comic store.
RATED
T
TEEN
viz media
www.viz.com
HOSHIN ENGI © 1996 by Ryu Fujisaki/SHUEISHA Inc.

SHONEN JUMP
100% NINJA ACTION!
SHONEN JUMP™
NARUTO™
NINJA COUNCIL 3
Available NOW!
exclusively for
NINTENDO DS™
Over 20 playable characters from the show.
Use the touch screen or microphone to unleash special jutsu.
4-player wireless head-to-head battles.
D3PUBLISHER
TOMY
RATING PENDING
RP
CONTENT RATED BY ESRB
Visit www.esrb.org for updated rating information.
火遁・
の
鳳仙火
NARUTO © 2002 MASASHI KISHIMOTO This product is manufactured, distributed and sold under license from VIZ Media, LLC. All Rights Reserved. Game and
©2006 TOMY. NINJA COUNCIL ™ and © 2002 TOMY. All Rights reserved. TOMY and its logo are trademarks of TOMY. VIZ Media and its logo are tradema
Media, LLC. SHONEN JUMP ™ and its logo are Trademarks of SHUEISHA, Inc. D3Publisher and its logo are trademarks of D3Publisher of America, Inc.
Nintendo DS are trademarks of Nintendo. © 2004 Nintendo. The ratings icon is a registered trademark of the Entertainment Software Association.

SUBSCRIBE TODAY & BECOME
MEMBER OF THE SHONEN JUM
SUBSCRIBER CLUB...
You'll get:
*Access to Exclusive Online Content!
*50% Savings Off the Newsstand Price!
*Exclusive Premiums!
All this available ONLY to Subscribers!
SHONEN JUMP
THE WORLD'S MOST POPULAR MANGA ™
FILL OUT THE SUBSCRIPTION CARD ON THE OTHER SIDE, OR SUBSCRIBE ONLINE AT:
www.shonenjump.com

Save 50% off the newsstand price!

SHONEN JUMP™

THE WORLD'S MOST POPULAR MANGA

SUBSCRIBE TODAY and SAVE 50% OFF the cover price PLUS enjoy all the benefits of the SHONEN JUMP SUBSCRIBER CLUB, exclusive online content & special gifts ONLY AVAILABLE to SUBSCRIBERS!

☑ **YES!** Please enter my 1 year subscription (12 issues) to *SHONEN JUMP* at the INCREDIBLY LOW SUBSCRIPTION RATE of $29.95 and sign me up for the SHONEN JUMP Subscriber Club!

Only $29^95!

NAME

ADDRESS

CITY [redacted] STATE [redacted]

E-MAIL ADDRESS

☐ MY CHECK IS ENCLOSED ☐ BILL ME LATER

CREDIT CARD: ☐ VISA ☐ MASTERCARD

ACCOUNT # EXP. DATE

SIGNATURE

CLIP AND MAIL TO

SHONEN JUMP
Subscriptions Service Dept.
P.O. Box 515
Mount Morris, IL 61054-0515

Make checks payable to: **SHONEN JUMP.**
Canada add US $12. No foreign orders. Allow 6-8 weeks for delivery.

P6SJGN YU-GI-OH! © 1996 by Kazuki Takahashi / SHUEISHA Inc.

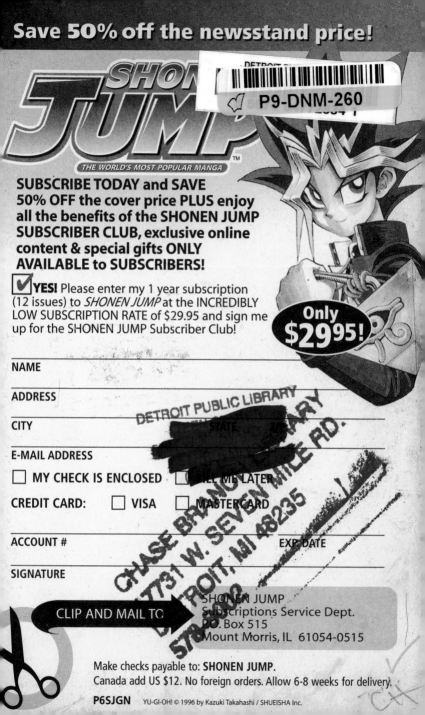